Those countries which "feed"
an educational system
with leftovers
will have to subsist
on leftovers as well.

ANATOLY GUIN

**Illustrations and Cover Design**
M. Yu. Larkin

**Translated by** Jennifer Sunseri, PhD

**Edited and adapted by** Mark G. Barkan, PhD

**Guin A., Barkan M.**
  SUCCESS FACTOR. Teaching Creative Thinking Skills. – Performance Press, Oak Ridge, TN USA, 2015 — 88 pp. Ill.

  ISBN 978-0-942442-32-8

  This book is for readers who are interested in developing their creative skills. The authors of the book have an extensive background in creative pedagogy and are known throughout the world as specialists in TRIZ, the theory and practice of inventive problem solving.

**Anatoly Guin, Mark Barkan**

# SUCCESS FACTOR

## TEACHING CREATIVE
## THINKING SKILLS

# CONTENTS

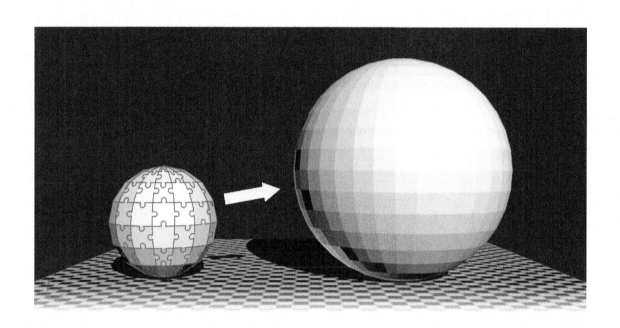

## FOREWORD FOR THE ENGLISH EDITION

Renowned physicist Leo Szilard proposed a simple, yet elegant image: Let's represent all human knowledge as a ball. Then the space outside of the ball is unknown territory. The surface of the ball symbolizes the border with the unknown. But the larger the amount of knowledge, the greater the area of contact with the unknown. And each point of the interface with the unknown is a problem that needs solving in order to acquire new knowledge.

In most cases, existing knowledge is insufficient to solve these problems. The ability to think is strongly required in order to deal with them. Thus, the more we as a society know the more thinkers/ problem solvers we need. And yet our schools fail at all levels when it comes to teaching creative and critical thinking skills.

The book you are about to read is dedicated to one of the most effective methods for teaching creative and critical thinking skills. The authors view this book as a primary guide for teachers and parents on how to teach solid thinking skills, and the exercises provided combine a variety of methods, with TRIZ being the main one, to help teachers and parents with this very difficult task.

Anatoly Guin
Mark Barkan

# REVIEWS

*Written in a lucid, breezy style, this book draws the reader in from the first pages and doesn't release him until the end. You'll keep on thinking as you read, "That's right! Really, right on target!" This is exactly what the educational curriculum needs!"*

*The book invites the reader to ponder what can be done so that children are passionate about their studies, so that they experience the excitement of solving non-standard open problems and the feeling of pride that comes with: "I've solved it! I did it myself!" Right now this is what we're lacking in our schools!*

*"The goal of a good education is to equip the individual with the ability to be useful, to live in harmony with others and the surrounding world. But this world is full of contradictions, and these can become problems or obstacles on the path of life, or else they can be challenges with a solution."*

*This book, though not lengthy, expresses the professional credo of the authors. One can only hope that open problems find their way into the school, and that the educational system will then be transformed into a valuable and interesting learning process for students.*

*Irina Osmolovskaya, Director of the Laboratory of Didactics
RAO Institute of Theory and History of Pedagogy,
Doctor of Pedagogical Sciences, Moscow, Russia.*

*You'll inhale this book, and from then on you'll be "infected" by open problems. This book is a wonderful motivator. The desire to change the content of education today, to change one's own thinking process, is gaining momentum. After participating in one of Anatoly Guin's seminars, teachers of history, biology, chemistry, introduced open problems to their students and received in return from the kids a huge interest in the study topic, as well as respect for the teacher. Given the option, students always choose open problems and never opt for traditional lessons!*

*For me, open problems have also increasingly become a tool for solving pedagogical problems: how to interest adolescent children (grades 6—8) in cognitive intellectual activity. At this age, it's important that children engage in finding themselves and obtaining intrinsic experience in various spheres along the lines of "what if ....?" Open problems let you feel like a discoverer.*

*What open problems create for students is an environment in which dialogue and healthy competition flourish, both of which are so important at this age. As the fear of unfamiliar real-life situations is banished, the psychological readiness for new "unknowns" develops.*

*Open problems are interesting for both children and adults. At teacher-parent meetings, our parents and teachers are happy to engage in creative problem solving with the children. Together, they find solutions to open problems.*

*As you read this book, you will find that you are not only a reader, but also a solver of open problems. And after you have read it, you will have to decide a vitally important issue: where, when and how you will implement open problems in your school community and among those whose development is of importance to you.*

*Elena Gredinarova, Director, Eidos School, Ph.D.,
Associate Professor, Department of Applied Psychology
Zaporizhzhya National University, Ukraine.*

*The authors actually disclose the secret of creative thought processes. The numerous real-life success stories make the book entertaining and easy to read. It facilitates the thinking process, and enhances the ability and desire to learn. I think this book is essential for teachers, parents and students.*

*Eng Hoo Ten, Senior Manager of Talent Development, Multimedia Development Corporation, Malaysia.*

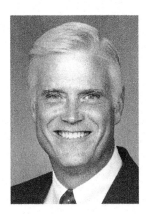

*This book is something new – it's not another book on the traditional approach to education. It encourages us to pay attention to changes in the content of education, to change the emphasis from teaching oriented toward assimilating facts to how to develop creative thinking. And it provides a clear understanding of this approach to learning – learning through open problems. The book serves as an excellent starting point for all educators interested in the development of creative thinking in children. I suspect that it will also help teachers of middle school students change the way they think, fostering their own creativity. This book will be useful for leaders in education who are concerned about the current status of the field.*

*Professor Lee Martin, University of Tennessee, Knoxville, USA.*

Either a country cares about educating
people to be creative,
or that country ends up looking to other
countries for new products and ideas.

# 5 reasons
## to read
## this book

- To be happy and successful, you need to be creative.
  This aspect of the world today is gaining momentum with each
  new day. This book lays out in a simple and engaging manner
  the most important tool for the development of creative thinking –
  open problems.

- If you are parents with pre-school or school-aged children, then you can unlock
  their potential.

- If you're a teacher, this book is a major step toward a creative style of teaching.

- If you're working in governmental education policy, the Theory of Inventive
  Problem Solving (TRIZ) gives you the opportunity to confront the single
  most important issue in the nation.

- If you're a person of wealth and a responsible citizen, you can make a mark
  on the history of your nation, or even contribute to all of humanity, by providing
  a portion of your resources to the development of human potential.

The key to the mystery of the golden fire awaits you in this book...

### The Golden Fire

*There once was a farmer in Siberia. One day at the market, he built a large log house, furnished it with wooden furniture, stacked firewood all around it, doused it with kerosene and set it on fire. This was in 1896, and he attracted a large crowd. As a result of this action, the farmer prospered.*
*How did he make this happen?*

This farmer had come up with something that had hitherto not existed – something that was useful for others. And he had found a way to communicate his discovery in a way that the people would understand. And finally, he was able to implement his invention and enrich himself. This was a creative person. However, countless other people started out with the same resources, knowledge, abilities, and they achieved nothing of the sort. Why not?

### The parable of the wise king and his creative courtier[1]

*Once the king of a great country decided to test his courtiers. He had to decide who among them was worthy of occupying an important post in his kingdom. He saw around him a group of strong, honorable men. "You are my worthy subjects," said the King, "I have for you a difficult problem, and I would like to know who among you is able to solve it." He displayed before them a huge padlock — of such a size as never before seen. "This is the largest and most complicated lock in my kingdom. Who among you can open it?" asked the King. Some of his courtiers shook their heads. Some began to examine the lock, but soon confessed that they, too, were unable to open it. And now that the honorable men had fallen short of the task, the other courtiers also admitted that they were not capable of it. But one young man stepped forth from the crowd and approached the lock. He began to carefully poke and prod it, and suddenly, with one jerk he opened it! It turned out that it had been unlocked all along! Then the king declared: "You are the one for the position, because you rely not only on what you see and hear, but also on your own abilities, and you are not afraid to try."*

The king was wise to seek out a man capable of bucking convention. This means that he found someone who would certainly be able to handle the creative problems that inevitably arise in important public positions. In short, he had determned which of these men was a creative person.

Some years ago, you already completed your first great accomplishment — you were born! We do not know what weight and height you were at birth. But we do know: you were a creative child.

How do we know this? Judge for yourself: as a newborn, you emerged into a completely unfamiliar realm – a brand new world! You knew absolutely nothing about its properties and hazards, and had no comprehension of the language spoken by the people. You need to survive, but to do this you need to learn how to comprehend, to aquire fundamental skills, to work through a wealth of new impressions. This is a very creative task and yes, you succeeded in mastering it!

Born with a huge potential for creating the new, a person, as a rule, loses this on the road of life, some to a greater, other to a lesser extent. Usually it is more, rather than less, that is lost. The famous American psychologist Abraham Maslow studied the biographies of highly creative people. This included "torturing" them with detailed questions. One of the takeaways Maslow came away with is this: "Children do not need to be taught curiosity. Children can be weaned from curiosity, and I think that this is the tragedy unfolding in our kindergartens and schools."[2]

---

[1] Quoted in V.A. Sonin, *Psikhologiya resheniya nestandartykh zadach*. [The Psychology of Nonstandard Problems.] Moscow: 2009

[2] Maslow, A.G. *Motivation and Personality*. SPb., 1999.

PROBLEM

**CLOSED**

**CLEAR CUT**

THE ONE
AND ONLY

**THE ONE AND ONLY**

CONDITIONS

*OPEN*

*FUZZY*

*SOLVING PROCESS*

MORE
THAN
ONE

*SOLUTIONS*

THE NUMBER
OF CONDITIONAL
SOLUTIONS

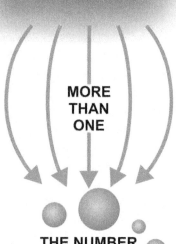

Curiosity, inquisitiveness – these provide fertile ground for the growth of creativity. And yet as soon as we are adults, we waste no time in contriving to destroy these traits. Why? If you observe a five-year child, you can already determine the extent to which his creativity has been extinguished. Or, conversely, to what extent it has been fostered and is flourishing.

> *When Christine was 6 years old, she was given a white rat. Beaming with joy, she took it with her on a walk with Daddy. But then Dad needed to drop into a store. He was clearly conflicted: it just wasn't right to go inside with a rat. A dialogue ensued between them:*
> *"Christine, sit on the bench with the rat while I dash into the store. I'll just be a minute."*
> *"Daddy, I want to go with you!"*
> *"You can't take Missy Rat into the store."*
> *"Then let Missy Rat sit on the bench while we go inside together ... we'll be fast ..."*
> *"Christine, you see that the rat is still tiny. She does not understand that she may fall off the bench. And if she falls, she will either break a leg, or get lost. So you'd better wait."*
> *(Satisfied that he was right, Daddy turned on his heel and started heading inside...)*
> *"Wait!" The girl put her rat on the bench and began to gently push it to the edge. At the edge, the creature began to balk. "You see!" said Christine triumphantly, "She already understands everything!"*

This 6-year-old girl already knows how to stand up for herself, make a case for her beliefs, and even conduct an experiment to support them. And this did not happen by itself. She learned these patterns of behavior at home.[3]

> *In the evening five-year-old David caught a butterfly and brought it home. But the butterfly suddenly flew off. There it goes, flying and spinning in the large, brightly lit room. What to do now? Maybe grab a net and swing it until you catch it again? But there are figurines, furniture, paintings on the wall all over the room – not a good idea. Call the grown-ups in for help?*
> *David turned off the lights in the room, found a flashlight and turned it on. "The butterfly will fly to the light, and I'll catch it."*

For this child he only did what was natural. He's used to the fact that life consists of problems to be solved using his head

Actually, there are two types of problems: closed and open.

Closed problems have well-defined parameters. All that is needed to solve the problem is within these parameters, and there is nothing outside of that. As a rule, there's only one way to solve them, and one correct answer. The educational system is structured predominately on solving problems such as these.[4] In fact, these are not even problems, as such. Rather, they are exercises that are designed to cultivate certain thinking skills, such as the skills used in applying formulas. But in life, these kinds of problems are virtually non-existent! And when they do come up, they are solved much faster by a computer than by a human being. Life is full of open problems. These have fuzzy, vague, conditions that are puzzling right to the end, and different approaches can be taken in their resolution. The answer to any one of these problems are potentially debatable, or even controversial. To build a new bridge, or a machine, to cure a person, to teach your child to think, and even to find the right partner in life — any of these endeavors requires the ability to see and solve open problems.

This book, then, is about open problems — the most important and versatile tool in developing creativity.

---

[3] The authors are not promoting the notion that an animal should be left unattended. The father of this creative girl must either himself be creative, or he might end up falling back on an authoritative approach – to the, detrimental to his relationship with his daughter.
[4] Yes, and university too, with the exception of certain progressive universities or "random" professors.

The world is changing rapidly. Education is falling behind just as fast.

Computers and other high-tech solutions in the classroom are not enough to rectify the situation. It is the content of education that must be changed. How?

Here we will focus on the transition of education from closed problems to open problems...

**Two case studies from the practice of Anatoly Guin**

It's time for the district physics Olympiad. 30 "tadpoles" — winners of their school competitions — are ready for battle. The assigned problems are distributed, the time passes... 20 minutes later I approach one clearly anxious boy — what's the matter?

"Well, I think I solved the problem, but I can't understand what the date has to do with it."

I read the problem[5]:

> In 1785, French balloonist Charles threw a stone from the basket of a balloon ascending at a speed of 1 m/s.
>
> How much time will it take the stone to reach the ground if it is thrown from a height of 300 m? Air resistance is negligible.

The task is simple, almost standard, but the boy is stumped by the "1785". He is accustomed to being given all the required conditions, and nothing more...

And now I am in a group of 16 physics teachers. I am giving them a "tricky" puzzle:

> How much will the water level in a tub change, if you toss a brick into it?

The first reaction is confusion: What kind of tub? What kind of brick? I say:

"Approximate the standard sizes."

After this almost everybody succeeds in tackling the problem in no time: water is displaced by the mass of the brick — problem solved!

I ask:

"And you've thought it over well?"

And someone else suddenly asks:

"What if the bath is full to the brim? Then the water level is the same – it just means some of it overflows!"

"Wonderful. Anything else?"

"Wait, wait!" There's palpable excitement in the audience – there might not be much water at all since, after all, it's not given how much there is in the problem...If the water doesn't totally cover the brick, then only as much of the brick as is submerged will displace the water. Knowing the depth of the water, we can calculate the amount...

"So," I summarize, "this task requires that you, yourself come up with the conditions, that you fill in the missing pieces. Now that you've thought about it, you've come up with three scenarios:

1.  When the water level falls below the size of the brick.
2.  When the water covers the brick, but the bath is not yet full.
3.  When the bath is full."

"This is an open problem. You managed to work out what it entails – the conditions. Now let's explore this open problem in greater depth."

"The conditions dictate that the brick will land in the tub. Let's think: How will the answer to the problem change depending on exactly how the brick is projected into the bath?"

The audience is excited:

"The brick could fly at high speed, and this will cause the water to splash out of the tub!"

"Or the brick could even bust a hole in the tub!"

---

[5] I'm citing these details from memory.

# PROBLEM SOLVING: WEAK AND STRONG

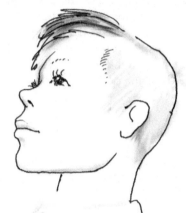

**When Mikey has a problem to solve:**

He doesn't stop to think,
He jumps right in, because for him
The main thing is to rush, rush, rush.

He wants to finish first, you see,
Because to him that means he's "best."
And when he doesn't have a clue,
He see what Google can help him do.

But when his ideas, so quickly found
Don't work? He gives up fast!
His mood is shot, his face turns black,
He gets upset, he turns his back.

*Poor Mikey! He isn't ready*
*For the challenges awaiting him in life.*

**When Eddie has a problem to solve:**

He takes the time to think it over,
Inside-out, and up-and-down.
Wikipedia? Google? No, instead,
The answers begin inside his head.

And if at first he doesn't win?
He tries again, and then again!
And if the problem's really hard,
He likes the challenge it presents.

To Eddie, there is no such thing as "failing",
Because when something doesn't work,
It just needs fixing.

*Eddie is a great problem solver, and as such,*
*He's equipped for life.*

THINK. LEARN. SUCCEED.

**EDUCATION**
FOR A NEW ERA

"The impact of the brick warms the water, and some part of it will evaporate!"

"What if the brick is already hot? After all, they didn't say anything about that! Then we can easily calculate how much water evaporates and how the level will change."

"And what kind of brick are we talking about? What types of bricks are there, anyway? Are some bricks lighter than water? We need to check an encyclopedia."

"Enough," I say. "Now you have a sense of this. Based on what we've learned, we can generate several completely traditional closed problems about 'a tub full of water and a brick,' and then derive the standard numerical solution for them."

## What kinds of problems do we solve?

The answer is simple – we solve the problems that we've been taught to solve. Schools teach us how to solve closed problems. The formula for closed problems: clearly-defined conditions + an approved method for deriving the only correct answer. Step to the left, or step to the right from the straight and narrow approved method (and therefore the "approved" way of thinking!), and your score is lowered.

Psychologists distinguish between two types of thinking: convergent (closed, non-creative) and divergent (open, creative). Some scholars refer to a personality type dominated by convergent thinking as "intellectual," while, in contrast, the divergent personality is "creative." The well-educated individual is ready to solve very complex problems, but first, someone had to establish parameters for them, and then outline how to solve them – meaning these are, in fact, "closed" problems. The creative person is able to see and to establish goals for herself, and aims to break out of the constraints imposed by the conditions. Of course, everyone has both intellectual and creative abilities, but to varying degrees. As students grow up, creative thinking fades. An overwhelming number of students end up conforming. They are wary of independence, they tend to move away from original thought, and are oriented instead toward spoon-fed, thoroughly processed and vetted information. The ambiguousness and variability of the conditions required by creative problem solving scares them.

## The problems that surround us

There is no area of human activity free of open problems. Technology, science, art, human relations ... Want some examples?

### The Cat and the Starlings (life at home)
*As soon as chicks in the birdhouse started chirping, the cat made his appearance, licking his chops, waiting for his chance. The boy who built this house for the starlings wanted to help the birds. And he came up with a way to completely prevent cats from reaching the birdhouse.*
*How?*[6]

### The Power of the Swordfish (the realm of science)
*How do fish and dolphins manage to move through dense water at a speed that is more typical for flight? For example, the swordfish allegedly reaches a speed of 130 km/h. In order to reach that kind of speed in the water, the fish needs to generate the power of a car engine!*
*Living creatures derive energy from oxidative processes. But fish are cold-blooded, and their body temperature is not much higher than the temperature of the water, at which oxygen, by the way, is dissolved in very small amounts. And so they simply can't generate the power to reach those speeds! We can assume that the fish somehow know how to significantly reduce water resistance.*
*How? For the time being, the question remains unanswered.*[7]

---

[6] The boy rapped a sheet of tinfoil all the way around tree trunk. the tree trunk with a ring made of tin. A problem from the book: Ivanov, G. I. *Formuly tvorchestva, ili Kak nauchit'sa izobretat'*. Moscow: 1994

[7] These problems have been provided by Irina Andrjeevskaya, a TRIZ specialist.

Students lose their motivation
in the chasm between real life
and the walls of the school –
despite the best efforts
of their teachers.

**Theft in Ancient Rome (social science)**

*When the feast has ended and the guests have dispersed, the host puts out the lights to save on oil. But the slaves then steal the remaining oil. What to do? Bear in mind that it's not a good idea to drain the oil, as in a proper house the lights must always be in a state of readiness.*[8]

**A Dancing Perspective (the artistic realm)**

*The director of a ballet has a dilema with one of the scenes: the hunters are supposed to disappear into the woods. He decides that he wants the visual effect to mirror reality, whereby the figures of the hunters diminish as they move into the forest. But the stage is of a modest size, and so the dancers are not able to shrink by moving into the distance. What to do?*[9]

Closed problems are encountered only in school. The problems presented by life are different:
How to avoid getting picked on by bullies?
How to meet a boy or girl?
Where to go from high school?
— …

If they are unable to cope with issues such as these, then teens find that not only they, but also the people around them suffer the consequences.

Life requires the ability to solve open problems, but at school, only closed problems are taught. This gap between the demands of life and the reality of school undercuts the students' eagerness to learn and the best efforts of teachers to sustain their interest.

## Talents - Dullards, or two more cases from the practice of A. Guin

Kolya, an inveterate C-student and disciplinary case, impressed me as a bright enough boy. After another conflict with the teacher, I had a private conversation with him

"Why should I respect her?" said Kolya. "She's had five years to bone up on this textbook in college, and she has an answer book, and I don't. Give me the answer book, and you'll see how smart I am…"

This kind of stereotype is quite typical. This is the payback for cookie-cutter traditional education, which simply fails to engage any child with a lively mind. How many capable students just don't fit into the mold and are lost in the process? We are talking about smart, active, dynamic kids who sometimes look at the lessons as essentially deficient. Many note how on paper those alleged to be "stupid" include the schoolboy Einstein, the schoolboy Mendeleev, the schoolboy Brodsky and other great thinkers — all in the same vein. The fact is that these students, with their free and open minds, simply did not fit into the "factory-school".

*Thomas Edison started having problems with his studies from the very first grade. He once said that "if we merge together two cups of water, we get one, only it has twice the volume" (although the topic was the fundamentals of mathematics: 1 + 1 = 2). These kinds of "fabrications" in the classroom, as well as his categorical refusal to participate in class, were extremely irritating to teachers, and after one of them called the boy an "addle-brained idiot" the indignant mother withdrew her son from school.*

---

[8] The approach taken by the ancient Romans: the oil in the lamps was topped up until the lamps were full, and then the lamps were checked before they were lit again. Plutarch. Table Talk. Leningrad, 1990.

[9] This problem came from the practice of Valentina Berezina, a TRIZ specialist. Here is the original solution: "I divided all the dancers into six groups according to their height. The tallest of the hunters performed closest to the viewers, and after them was the second group of hunters, with the next shortest group behind them, and so on, until the procession was completed on the bridge by hunters of the smallest stature, which were portrayed by children. The illusion was so great that it seemed to the audience that the same six people were traveling on different paths of the forest. Along with this, the music matched the action, gradually fading and then falling silent… And even the colors of the costumes worn by the artists were more and more faded." Noverre, Jean-Georges. *Letters on Dancing and Ballet* Leningrad - Moscow, 1965.

WE ARE CREATIVE

we are excited about wonders of nature,

contradictions and paradoxes

we are interested in everything new,

unknown, not understood

we want to make life better

we can solve, invent, achieve

THINK. LEARN. SUCCEED.

EDUCATION FOR A NEW ERA

*Thus, the formal education of Thomas lasted only a few months, and further on he studied independently under the guidance of his mother (and consequently Edison could say, somewhat smugly, that he "became an inventor because in childhood he didn't go to school").[10]*

Sasha is a student in my new 8th-grade class.[11] Sasha appears to be a "hopeless" blockhead. On a test, I gave him a few questions and a textbook with which to find answers and write them down. He couldn't handle it — he couldn't find the right topic. Later on, I learn that, to my surprise, Sasha is considered a "moped specialist" who can take apart and repair an engine. That doesn't fit the image of a blockhead, does it?

I want to get to the bottom of this, sort it out, I befriend him. And that's what it is – an advanced case of a complete lack of motivation. In school he's killing time, and in real life, he's an overachiever.[12] Why?

The constant "taming" of free-thinking creative children, the attempt to force them to think in patterns leads some children to close themselves off. You may ask: What can we do about this? After all, these templates are essentially the rules for considering, deciding, and even formulating thoughts, and they can be very useful! Of course. Undoubtedly. Just as no doubt you need a roof on your house. But if it's close to the head and prohibits you from standing up, what you'll end up with is a curved spine or else a hole in the roof...

*The teacher assigned a problem on a test: Find a way to measure the height of a skyscraper using only a barometer. When checking the work, the teacher found that many students correctly understood how to use a barometer to determine height: you measure the air pressure on the ground floor and then on the top floor. However, one of the students wrote: Since he knows that the mercury in the glass tube of the barometer measures thirty inches, he measured the length of the shadow of the barometer and the shadow of the building, and could therefore calculate the height of the latter using proportions.*

*The next day, the teacher took this student aside and said:*

*"I can't say that you didn't provide a correct answer to the problem, but just the same, this is the case. I had in mind an aneroid barometer, but you solved the problem based on the assumption the barometer was mercury. Now that you know what I wanted, how would you answer the question?"*

*Without hesitation, the boy replied:*

*"I would climb to the roof of the building, throw the barometer off, and time how long it took for it to reach the ground. Then, by calculating the speed of a falling object, I would get the answer."*

*"Again, you are both right and wrong," said the teacher. "Try again, assuming that you do not have a watch."*

*"Well, then, I would locate the building's caretaker and tell him: 'If you tell me how tall this building is, I will give you this barometer.'"[13]*

This boy is inherently creative. Imagine him ending up in a school where he is penalized twice for each original solution. Or else he is given encouragement only for actions taken strictly according to the established pattern, which, in principle, amounts to the same thing. What will a few years of this do to him? Will he love school or will he do his utmost to resist schooling? This last question is, of course, rhetorical. We know what will happen. We see this in today's public schools. Caged birds never do learn how to fly...

---

[10] Ershov, K. *Starik i ego masterskaya* [*The Old Man and his Workshop*]. Chief Time, 04.2011.
[11] The events depicted occurred in 1981.
[12] Little by little we have been able to correct this situation. Sasha graduated from 8th grade with an A- GPA.
[13] This case is described in J.I. Nirenberg *Iskusstvo tvorcheskogo myshleniya* [*The Art of Creative Thinking*]. Mn., 1996.

## Docile Problems

You could say that there are two kinds of problems: Docile and Wild.
Docile problems are always predictable.
To solve them, all you need is a firm grasp of the rules and formulas.

Wild problems are an art.
They are crafty,
and hunting them requires
a fair amount of ingenuity.

In this chapter,
we try to bring some order
into the world of wild problems
by putting them in categories.

Wild problems

The inventive Problem
puts in front of those
who would solve
it the question "How can this be?"
when additional conditions make the obvious
solution impossible, when the intelligent
application of traditional knowledge
(skills, experience ...) is inadequate

Creative thinking can be fostered and developed to unlock each person's full potential. However, for this we need to change the content of education. Instead of rapidly aging facts, we need to be teaching ways of thinking, as well as the practical application of any solutions. In other words, we need to be teaching how to solve creative problems across a wide range of knowledge. We first introduced open problems a quarter of a century ago. Our successes have demonstrated the effectiveness of this approach to fostering creativity in young minds. With open problems, those ubiquitous facts (concepts, terms, formulas, scientific principles), that need to be memorized are much more easily assimilated. This is because when students apply themselves to solving open problems, when they engage in intellectual and creative activity of a high order, they see for themselves that the facts they need are best accessed and directed at the task at hand when they are in their heads rather than pulled off the Internet.

Thus, the education system must embrace open problems. They come in different types, and so we'll specify them by category, much like a zoologist describes animals by species and family. We'll begin with the **_inventive problem._**

Let's imagine the following situation: You want to eat. On the table in front of you is bread. What to do? The answer is obvious, for now there is no problem. But then we add additional conditions: We see at the table a hungry lion. He also wants to eat ,and he's waiting for you to approach the bread. Now what to do? This is clearly a problem that requires _ingenuity_ ...

We see that the **_inventive problem_** solver poses the question "What to do?" when additional conditions render the obvious solution null and void, when the intelligent application of traditional knowledge (skills, experience, ...) is insufficient.

### The "military feint" with potatoes[14]

_Potatoes are poisonous  – this was what certain French physicians of the 18th century affirmed. Potatoes made it to France by way of America, and their reception by the French population was guarded. Even the famous Big Encyclopedia, which was published in 1765 by the leading French scholars – Didetot, D'Alembert, and others – reported that potatoes were course, fit only for unrefined bellies._

_Nevertheless, the famous French agronomist Antoine-Augustin Parmentier set out to cultivate them in French fields, because for many ordinary people this would be their escape from hunger. However, his attempts to prove the benefits of potatoes to the people fell on deaf ears – the peasants stubbornly refused to grow potatoes. Parmentier then realized that he needed a gimmick._

_Come up with various ways to interest people in potatoes._

This, too, is an inventive problem. The standard solutions – persuasion, explanation, promotional activities – simply didn't work. Why they didn't work is a different issue. Apparently, the distrust of the populace toward the elite was insurmountable. Any suggestions from "on high" were not well-received. So let us see how Parmentier got around these obstacles.

_In 1787, Parmentier was granted permission from the king to plant potatoes in a field that, at his request, was guarded by a contingent of the royal guard. But this was only during the day – at night the guard was removed. And then the people, attracted by the 'forbidden fruit,' began to steal into the field at night to dig up the potatoes, which they subsequently planted in their own gardens._

And this was how the ingenious agronomist solved his inventive problem, i.e. how to disseminate the potato to the people in the face of their rejection of it.[15] Of course, this is not the only possible solution, and you are free to come up with others.

---

[14] This problem was provided by the TRIZ specialist Irina Andrjeevsky.

[15] A monument was erected in France to Parmentier that bears the inscription: "Benefactor of humankind." One of the stations of the Paris Metro is named after the agronomist. And French cooking immortalized his name with a special potato soup, named, appropriately, Potage Parmentier.

When something
is ambiguous or incomprehensible,
the questions to ask
are "Why?", "How?", "What are the reasons?"

People often think that inventions involve a lot of engineers and technicians. In fact, problems like these have required solving throughout human history, everywhere, always, in virtually every sphere of life. These kinds of problems are a constant in the life of the individual. But education and culture do not teach people to see these problems. For most adults, life presents itself as a succession of events, both good and bad. Only a clear minority, those with heightened creativity, knows how to transfer personal experiences to the task, thereby finding a solution that translates into success. That being said, frequently observers of the creative individual attribute her success to simple luck.

### Letter to the newspaper: Please advise![16]

*A couple of months ago, I fell ill. The doctor recommended that I undergo an examination at the hospital. It turned out that I was just tired and there were no serious health problems. But there are worrisome rumors making their way around the office along the lines of "he's seriously ill, and a new boss will be stepping in to replace him." I really don't like this, because this kind of talk gets in the way of work. On top of this, I'm not prone to publicly discussing my health.*
*I would appreciate any advice on how I should address this situation.*

*Michael T. owner of a printing company.*

This is an example of an everyday problem from the workplace. This is not a complicated issue, and we invite the reader to come up with solutions. Why even think about this seemingly mundane issue here? It is a slice of life, that's why, and without creativity, it can seem far more problematic than it is. Indeed, people are often at a loss with these kinds of issues related to their everyday wellbeing. They might opt to ignore them, or else they worry about them and complain, but don't address them head on. The creative person, however, takes them in stride – it's all part of life!

A relative of the ***inventive problem*** is the ***design problem***. In addition to the actual solution, a ***design problem*** requires the provision of a means of implementing the solution. For example:

### Save the life of the pilot

*In the event of an emergency, the pilot of military aircraft can take advantage of the catapult. The catapult ejects the pilot from the cockpit upwards, the parachute is activated, and thus, the pilot is saved from certain death. But if a catapult like this was mounted on a combat helicopter, the pilot would be launched right into the propeller blades, thus nullifying this solution.*
*What to do? Can you think of a way to save the life of a combat helicopter pilot?*

In addition to this, there is the ***research problem***. This kind of problem arises when something incomprehensible must be made clear to someone , meaning a certain phenomenon that occurs or is currently happening. It needs to be explained, but how? What are the causes of the phenomenon? Usually the conditions to the problem presuppose an entire set of responses/hypotheses. This is how it happens in science. Any phenomenon is first described, then there are various hypotheses to explain the phenomenon. Then, these hypotheses are discussed, verified. Thus, in addressing open research problems, real science takes shape and undergoes development.

### The Dancing Drop of Water

*If a drop of water falls onto a hot surface, it usually evaporates quickly. However, if the surface is extremely hot, the drop will slide, "dance" on the surface, and at the same time it will take much longer to evaporate.*
*What is the explanation for this amazing fact?*

---

[16] Elityi personnel, No. 8 (394), 03/01/2005.

Seeing the unusual in the usual —
this skill is the purview of creative people.
And just like any other skill
it can be developed.

The "dancing drop" is the kind of scientific problem that high school students can solve. By the way, this phenomenon is easy to demonstrate in school and even at home.

Any observation, in fact, can serve as the source of educational research problems. For example, a typical child's question: Why don't clouds fall to earth since they consist of water, which is heavier than air? This is a great research problem, although it's not particularly simple.

### The Eternal Clock

*In one European museum, there is a clock that has functioned without winding for two centuries. How is this possible?*

Here are some answers/hypotheses proposed by students:

- The clock is recharged by hidden wires from the wind turbine on the roof;
- It runs off the power generated by visitors opening the door;
- Its operation is powered by atmospheric pressure: a box like the one that is used in an aneroid barometer is all that's required. As the pressure increases, the box shrinks, and winds the clock's spring (this phenomenon is studied in physics classes);
- It's the same phenomenon whereby human hair frizzes in humid weather;
- The clock is simply an exhibition, that is, it doesn't really work, doesn't show the correct time.

The solution to problems like this develops creative skills in children and teaches them to look at things and phenomena from different angles, to see the unusual in the usual. Moreover, when solving problems such as these, students no longer feel that there are things that aren't worth knowing. This is because when working on specific problems any knowledge from any source – physics, chemistry, biology, geography – might apply. Indeed, this is the case for science as a whole. It's no coincidence that the great scientists generally have all had wide-ranging educations.

A research problem can be culled from anywhere, essentially.

### Death Defying Acts

*"He stepped out into the arena, bowed in the traditional Japanese fashion with his hand pressed to his belly, then he threw his light gray kimono off, revealing short leotards and bare, athletic arms His assistant was heating a large ladle on a brazier after first throwing pieces of some kind of metal into it – most likely tin or lead. And when the metal was melted, she makes the round of the arena with the spoon, showing the audience the molten metal in the smoldering spoon, liquid and smooth as cream.*

*She proffers the spoon toward the Japanese performer, leaning toward him in a deep ritual bow; with a sharp movement he brings the red-hot spoon to his mouth, pours the molten metal in, and some time later, in full view of the public, spits out pieces of solidified metal, which, one after another fall with a clink onto the tray held before him. This was astounding, and the entire circus erupts in applause ..."[17]*

*Explain how a person can ingest molten metal into his mouth.*

Whatever idea or hypothesis is postulated as a solution to this problem requires verification.

---

[17] Kataev, V.P. Broken Life, or the Magic Horn of Oberon. Moscow: 1973

The real problem
solver asks "Why"
and launches a study to find out.
Next he asks "What if..."
and proceeds to find a solution.

This can be a calculation or experiment. In many cases, the verification can be done through reasoning, as a thought experiment. In a thought experiment, we think over a variety of consequences of what would happen if our hypothesis is correct. For example, in solving the problem "Death Defying Acts," high school students all assumed it was some kind of metal with a very low melting point. An Internet search led to the hypothesis that it was gallium – a metal with a melting point of about 30 degrees Celsius. That is, it can be melted right in your hands!

But then we had the students conduct a thought experiment: What would happen if you actually poured gallium in your mouth? A study of the properties of the metal showed that it is very toxic, and therefore it simply isn't possible to use gallium in this trick. This means that the hypothesis is false and we must look elsewhere for a solution ... [18]

A thought experiment such as this is in fact an example of a solution to this cateory of problem – an **expert level problem**. Let's take a look at another example of this species of problem.

### That's a spade, not a gun!

*In 1940, one of the junior officers of the Soviet army came up with an idea for "improving" the sapper spade He suggested that instead of a wooden handle, a steel pipe could be used through which you could shoot shells. That is, you can turn the shovel into a mortar. They conveyed his idea right to the commander in chief! Come up with arguments "for" and "against" this innovation.*

*What do you think, was it implemented as a weapon?*

The solution to this problem can be found in the pages of history and through a study of the technical characteristics of mortar weapons and sapper spades, especially their application.

> *The spade-mortar was not put into service. Tests showed that the adaption made the spade too heavy, and thus awkward to use. At the same time, it was still not heavey enough to be used as a mortar, and so even if light, ineffective shells were employed, it could not be reliably used to hit a target. Incidentally, expert gunners warned about this before testing was launched.*

A **forecast** can be thought of as a subcategory of the expert problem. A forecast problem is usually focused on the future, when the effects are distant and an empirical test is not possible.

### Onward, to the Caves!

*Minerals are often mined deep underground. Once the mining is over, huge caverns are left behind.*

*How can people make use of these underground spaces?*

Possible hypotheses (from high school students):

• People can deliberately set off a cave-in, the way they trigger snow avalanches so that they aren't accidentally set off; this would correspond to a new profession related to shaping the environment...

• Perhaps the caves could be used for storing industrial waste, thus freeing up useful land on the surface of the Earth;

• If you think about what to dump and in what order, then many years later, when the wastes have "fermented," our descendants can make use of the resulting stores of useful minerals;[19]

• The caves can be used for tourism;

• You can transform them into spaces for factories, plants, or, museums ...

---

[18] Incidentally, this metal simply won't harden inside one's mouth as the temperature in this orifice is above 30º C.
[19] This idea is from a book by the founder of TRIZ, Genrich. S. Altshuller.

The immediate future
is rife with unresolved
open problems.
Our quality of life
will depend on the quality
of the decisions we make

This chapter extends our classification of open problems, which is, by the way, like any other classification scheme, relative. It does not include the full range of problems – only those that the authors regard as the most representative.[20]

In fact, any problem with a high degree of openness may include different types of intellectual and creative activities, and contain subtasks that involve inventiveness, research, and expertise. For example, the following problem:

### The Fire in the Skyscraper

*A fire in a residential building is always very dangerous. But it's especially lethal if it is in the upper floors of a skyscraper.*

*Propose solutions that will prevent casualties and minimize losses from fires in skyscrapers.*

This problem is multifaceted. Humanity has yet to come up with a uniform solution. The conditions for the problem do not stipulate from which perspective it is to be tackled. Thus, one must seek solutions from the prespective of construction companies, from fire services, from residents of upper floors, and from the public as a whole. The quest for ideas could require excursions into engineering, architecture, physics and chemistry, psychology, and many other realms of knowledge.

A serious solution to a problem such as this could be converted into an extensive team project. First, you need to analyze the conditions and gather information on the topic. You need to elucidate possible causes of fires, the risk factors, examine the standard solutions that have already been applied in this sphere. This requires solutions to a few **expert problems** to discern the shortcomings of existing solutions. This also requires a **research problem** that tackles the hidden, rare and unusual causes of fires to ensure a comprehensive list is compiled. Then, an **inventive problem** directed at the conditions needs to be solved. After this, try to make a **forecast**: How will we fight fires in the distant future? A number of the ideas generated by the solutions can be verified by an additional information search, or by conversations with scientists in the field, or through experiments.

---

[20] The authors have developed another, much more wideranging classification with numerous parameters of open problems displayed in a morphological table.

Mathematics teachers know how often children obtain meaningless results when solving common problems involving calculations. For example, "one and a half diggers did the job." Mathematics at school is very far removed from its original function, i.e., meeting practical needs. The problems and their solutions are often "outside of real life".

For some children, learning math seems like nothing more than a hopeless competition with a calculator. The fact is that nowadays, math courses teach formal mathematical operations. And you need to learn to use mathematics, that is, to construct a model of the problem. This model then lets students apply a formula to make the calculation.

### The Wave Runner[21]

*Frezi stood, biting her lip. As luck would have it, the young lieutenant got it into his head to tell her a compliment.*

*"You are so light," he said, "that if you wanted to you could run to that island atop the waves without getting your feet wet."*

*"Have it your way, sir," she said. And from wave to wave, jumping and leaping, Frezi Grant ran to the island.*

*Estimate how fast she would have to run in order to avoid drowning.*

Try to come up with the calculation and solve this problem. To solve this problem, all you need is a command of high school level physics and mathematics. However, we witnessed genuine anxiety when we suggested to a group of physics teachers that they attempt it. In the conditions laid out for this problem, they did not see the usual formulas, because they, too, were not taught how to construct a model.

And, moreover, the model for this problem is not so simple. Our longterm experience has shown that adults with higher education often give up when confronted with even simpler tasks. They simply don't understand how the formulas they all know so very well can be applied to such a broadly formulated problem.

And yet ... As a rule, in school, problems requiring the exact same calculations are taught. These are closed problems, and in solving them, people are essentially duplicating a computer. More often than not, life requires us to assess things, to make approximate calculations. How much food to take on a hike, or gas on a trip? How much money is enough money to last? The number of leaflets for a promotional campaign, or buses required for a city? The list goes on and on. In engineering and science problems, the value of such approximate calculations using a simplified model has always been very high.

### From the memoirs of cosmonaut Alexei Leonov:[22]

*Academic Mstislav Keldysh[23] was an amazing person. He calculated the trajectories of spacecraft that delivered equipment to the moon. Once an automatic orientation system failed to function on board a ship, and there was an urgent need to calculate the parallax. The head computer programmer ran to his computer to calculate the answer, while Keldysh started scribbling something on a pack of cigarettes with his pencil. In a minute, he said, "Twenty meters." Half an hour later, the head of the computing center rushed back in, panting, and shouted enthusiastically, "We've got the answer – twenty meters!"*

---

[21] The subject matter of this problem is from A.S. Grin Begushaya po volnam [Running on Waves]. Moscow: 1980
[22] The first man to conduct a space walk in open space.
[23] A scientist and engineer, a groundbreaking thinker in Soviet science and chief theorist for the Soviet space program.

The ability to simplify a problem
is of colossal importance,
as is the ability to build a model
for which a solution is feasible.
Building a model is the first step
in transforming a real-life situation
into a problem.
This is what the school does not teach.
The school teaches problems
that someone has already formulated
and written down
in an easily digestible format.

That's how quickly and reliably an approximate result can be obtained – the aerial acrobatics of a creative mind! Thus in ancient times, Thales measured the height of the pyramid of Cheops, and Eratosthenes – the radius of the globe; and in recent times Enrico Fermi[24] reproduced the effect of a nuclear bomb on the armed forces by estimating the power of a nuclear explosion using scraps of paper. Fermi was among the scientists and military personnel watching the explosion at a great distance from the epicenter. He tossed the pieces of paper into the air when the much-weakened shock wave reached the observation post. For him, all he had to do was measure the distance that the wave carried the scraps of paper.

Problems such as these, which require the construction of a model and a sample calculation, are called **assessments.** In our experience, many **research** or **inventive problems**, after they have been solved at the theoretical level, then move into the assessment phase if there is a need to verify the hypotheses with a calculation.

### Strange Stones in Death Valley[25]

*California's Death Valley is a dried up lake surrounded by mountains. The clay bottom of the former lake is an almost perfectly smooth surface. Here, race car drivers frequently can be seen training and competing. Rain in the valley is a rarity, so the soil there is almost always hard, and special tracks for racing are not required. It would seem like you could drive in any direction and not have to think about anything. But here's the rub: on the smooth surface of the former lake bottom, even away from the surrounding mountains, there are single stones weighing up to 300 kg [640 lbs] These are deadly obstacles for drivers traveling at extremely high speeds.*

*Researchers in Death Valley found that the stones had fallen onto the surface of what had been the bottom of the lake after it had dried up. But they could not understand how the stones got there. Those with a mystical inclination attribute this phenomenon to intervention by supernatural forces.*

*Try to explain how the stones ended up on the surface of the lake so very far from the mountains. Bear in mind that any rock that falls from a mountain cannot simply roll that far.*

We tackled this problem many times both with adult audiences, and with high school students. Children usually propose 7–10 ideas with varying degrees of probability. Here are some of them:
- The stones were spewn by volcanoes;
- These are meteorites;
- Stones were transported there by people, perhaps for some kind of religious ritual;
- The stones emerged from below ground;
- At first the stones rolled down from the mountain, and then they were moved by strong winds.

A further analysis of the conditions and a search for information about Death Valley, itself, provides support to the probability that the last scenario is the most likely hypothesis. After all, in the valley there are high winds accompanied by rainfall, which makes the clay slippery. But this, in turn, leads us to ask: Can this wind, even given the slippery clay, move heavy stones? You can easily simulate these conditions in an experiment. All you need is a small stone, and a hair dryer or a vacuum cleaner to generate the wind. But how about large stones? For that, a calculation is needed. In high school, the students have sufficient knowledge to construct a model and calculate the possible outcome.[26]

But now we have to ask: Does the school teach this important skill? The answer is — no!
Is it possible to teach children how to solve problems like these?
The answer is — yes! This should begin with children in elementary school.

---

[24] Winner of the Nobel Prize in Physics.
[25] This problem is from A.A. Guin, A.F. Kavtrev. *Obyasnit' neobyasnimoe* [*Explaining the Inexplicable*]Moscow: 2012
[26] To back up this assertion, we provide the calculation in Appendix № 4.

Nature is unified.
But our study of it is disjointed.
This makes it easier, which is good.
But what's bad is that we're
violating the integrity of the paradigm,
i.e., the natural order.
Open problems are a solution
to this contradiction.

**The school's pine grove**

*Imagine that they decided to create a small pine grove in the schoolyard consisting entirely of fuzzy green firs. They elected to plant the grove on a plot of land the size of a classroom.*

*How many firs should they buy?*

Problems requiring ***assessments*** are much more interesting to children, and also more natural and closer to reality. They are easy to think up on the fly, while conducting lessons. For example, we decided to hold an exhibition of drawings done by the kids in class. How much wall space do we need? Solutions to problems like these teach children to think through to the end result of their activities. This means that it makes them more aware of what they do.

The artificial division of the study of holistic nature into individual subjects not only has obvious advantages, but also very significant disadvantages. Open problems are a solution to this inherent contradiction in the traditional system of education. They are tools that facilitate the processing and application of spheres of knowledge in their natural unity. When you are confronted with a new problem, you never know exactly what area of knowledge at your command will help you find the best solution.

*Once, the great American inventor Edison asked the mathematician Francis Upton to calculate the volume of a light bulb. Upton was a good mathematician, and about an hour later, he finished his calculations. After this, Edison measured the volume of the bulb in a few seconds —he simply used a beaker of water.*

This chapter should leave you with one simple conclusion: if you know how to calculate propblems, what this means is that you're able to apply mathematics in a variety of everyday, professional, and scientific contexts, i.e, to use your abilities in various situations, to ***make assessments***. If the mathematics you are taught does not provide you with these abilities, then it is eviscerated and essentially useless outside the schoolroom .

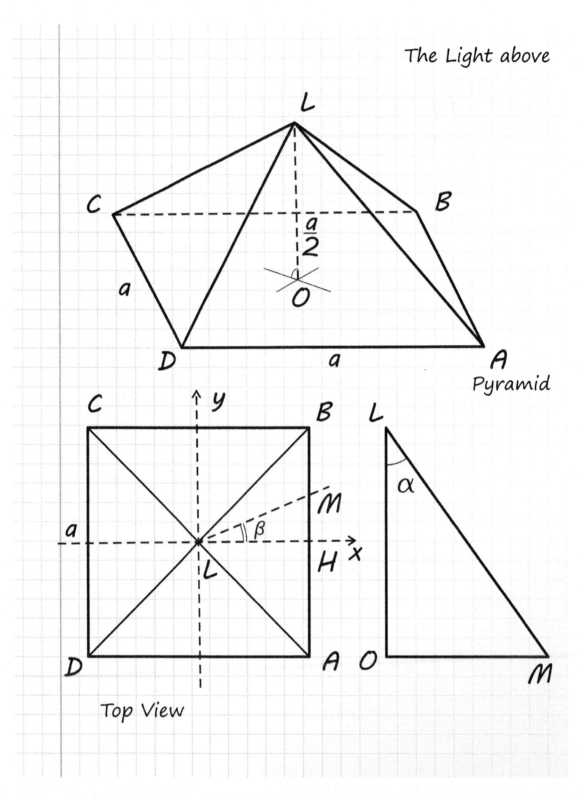

The Light above

Pyramid

Top View

On the drawings, the spherical coordinates represent any point M on the plot of land

How do students in grade school or high school feel when they can't solve a problem? More often than not, they experience apprehension.

How about in real life, when a man or a woman confronts a new challenge? Better still, what if his fate or her career hinges on the right resolution to this challenge?

We interviewed 25 students and graduates of prestigious universities. One said: "I feel excitement." The rest confessed that their first emotion was fear. This fear, of course, can subsequently be overcome. And then there is the simple fact that the more you practice non-standard problems the easier it is to cope with fear.

Fear causes people to avoid problems, close their eyes to new challenges – and in the process – to new opportunities. And it's not just fear that hinders good problem solving. If a person doesn't have the experience, if she is not in the habit of dealing with real-life situations (or the conditions inherent in open problems) from different angles, in different contexts, if she lacks a variety of intellectual tools and if she is simply uninterested in such matters, then one can hardly expect good results.

One day we asked a university professor to solve the following problem:

### The Light above the Playground
*A square playground with a length a, illuminated by a 100-watt light bulb. It hangs exactly in the middle of the playground, at a height of a/2. How much of the light being cast illuminates the playground, and what is spent on lighting the rest of the universe? Assume that light shines on all sides equally.*

Unfortunately, the professor had a good command of mathematics. At the next meeting, he provided a solution which had cost him a few hours of effort:

*The light bulb and the playground form a quadrangular pyramid ABCDL. At the base of the pyramid is a square ABCD with side a, the height of the pyramid LO is equal to a/2. As the light shines from point L in all directions equally, in order to solve the problem, first, the size of the solid angle at the vertex L and its ratio to the total solid angle must be found.*

*Consider the spherical system of coordinates $(\rho; \alpha; \beta)$:*

*Let us assume that $\beta \in [0; 2\pi]$.*

*From the condition $OL = \dfrac{a}{2}, OH = \dfrac{a}{2}$.*

*$OM = OL \bullet \mathrm{tg}\,\alpha$, but because $OM = \dfrac{OH}{\cos \beta}$, means,*

*$\alpha = \mathrm{arctg}\,\dfrac{OH}{\cos \beta \bullet OL} = \mathrm{arctg}\,\dfrac{1}{\cos \beta} \; for \; \beta \in \left[0; \dfrac{\pi}{4}\right].$*

*Then for the formula of the solid angle for an arbitrary spanning surface we have:*

$$\Omega = 8 \bullet \int_0^{\pi/4} \int_0^{\mathrm{arctg}\frac{1}{\cos\beta}} \sin\alpha \, d\alpha \, d\beta = 8 \bullet \int_0^{\pi/4} \left( \cos 0 - \cos\left( \mathrm{arctg}\,\dfrac{1}{\cos\beta} \right) \right) d\beta =$$

$$= 8 \bullet \int_0^{\pi/4} \left( 1 - \cos\left( \mathrm{arctg}\,\dfrac{1}{\cos\beta} \right) \right) d\beta$$

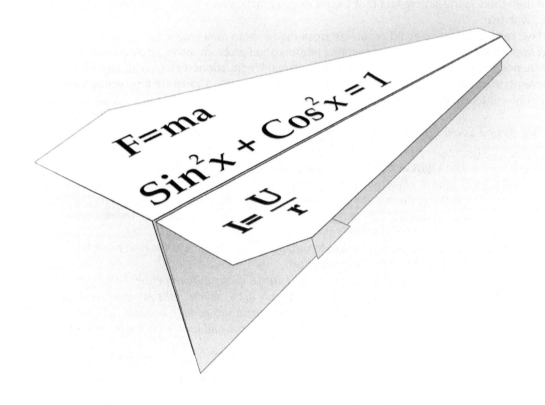

"Do I need to know the formula by heart?"

"Not if you are only trying to solve simple problems, which really aren't problems at all. Then, you can just check the answer book."

"But yes, you do, if you want to move beyond simple problems."

We know that $\cos\dfrac{x}{2}=\sqrt{\dfrac{1+\cos x}{2}}$, then

$$\int_0^{\pi/4}\left(1-\cos\left(\text{arctg}\,\frac{1}{\cos\beta}\right)\right)d\beta=\int_0^{\pi/4}\left(1-\cos\left(\frac{1}{2}\bullet 2\bullet\text{arctg}\frac{1}{\cos\beta}\right)\right)d\beta$$

$$=\int_0^{\pi/4}\left(1-\sqrt{\frac{1+\cos\left(2\bullet\text{arctg}\dfrac{1}{\cos\beta}\right)}{2}}\right)d\beta=A_1(\beta).$$

Let $\sqrt{\dfrac{1-x}{1+x}}=\dfrac{1}{\cos\beta}\Rightarrow\dfrac{1-x}{1+x}=\dfrac{1}{\cos^2\beta}$;

$1+x=\cos^2\beta-x\bullet\cos^2\beta$;

$x\bullet\left(\cos^2\beta+1\right)=\cos^2\beta-1$;

$x=\dfrac{\cos^2\beta-1}{\cos^2\beta+1}$.

Using the relationship $\arccos x=2\bullet\text{arctg}\sqrt{\dfrac{1-x}{1+x}}$, we obtain:

$$\cos\left(2\bullet\text{arctg}\frac{1}{\cos\beta}\right)=\cos\left(2\bullet\text{arctg}\sqrt{\frac{1-x}{1+x}}\right)=\cos\left(\arccos(x)\right)=x=\frac{\cos^2\beta-}{\cos^2\beta+}$$

$$A_1(\beta)=\int_0^{\pi/4}\left(1-\sqrt{\frac{1+\dfrac{\cos^2\beta-1}{\cos^2\beta+1}}{2}}\right)d\beta=$$

$$=\int_0^{\pi/4}\left(1-\sqrt{\frac{\dfrac{\cos^2\beta+1+\cos^2\beta-1}{\cos^2\beta+1}}{2}}\right)d\beta=\int_0^{\pi/4}\left(1-\sqrt{\frac{2\bullet\cos^2\beta}{2\bullet\left(\cos^2\beta+1\right)}}\right)d\beta$$

$$=\int_0^{\pi/4}\left(1-\sqrt{\frac{\cos^2\beta}{\cos^2\beta+1}}\right)d\beta.$$

But $\cos^2\beta+1=2-\sin^2\beta$;

$$A_1(\beta)=\int_0^{\pi/4}\left(1-\sqrt{\frac{\cos^2\beta}{2-\sin^2\beta}}\right)d\beta=\int_0^{\pi/4}\left(1-\frac{\cos\beta}{\sqrt{2-\sin^2\beta}}\right)d\beta.$$

We apply the following change $\beta$ through F:

let $F(\beta)=\sin\beta$; Then $F'(\beta)=\cos\beta\bullet d\beta$.

As a result of the substitution, the boundaries of the integration are changed:

$0\le\beta\le\dfrac{\pi}{4}$; $\sin 0\le\sin\beta\le\sin\dfrac{\pi}{4}$;

$0\le\sin\beta\le\dfrac{\sqrt{2}}{2}$; $0\le F\le\dfrac{\sqrt{2}}{2}$.

The first thing to understand
is that mathematics is an art.

*Paul Lockhart. A Mathematician's Lament*

$$A_1(\beta) = \int_0^{\pi/4}\left(1 - \frac{F'(\beta)}{\sqrt{2 - F^2(\beta)}}\right)d\beta = \int_0^{\pi/4}(1)d\beta - \int_0^{\pi/4}\left(\frac{F'(\beta)}{\sqrt{2 - F^2(\beta)}}\right)d\beta =$$

$$= \frac{\pi}{4} - \int_0^{\frac{\sqrt2}{2}}\frac{1}{\sqrt{2 - F^2}}dF = \frac{\pi}{4} - \left(\arcsin\frac{\sqrt2}{2\sqrt2} - \arcsin\frac{0}{\sqrt2}\right) =$$

$$= \frac{\pi}{4} - \left(\arcsin\frac{1}{2} - \arcsin 0\right) = \frac{\pi}{4} - \left(\frac{\pi}{6} - 0\right) = \frac{\pi}{12}.$$

*Thus,* $\Omega = 8 \bullet \dfrac{\pi}{12} = \dfrac{2\pi}{3}.$

*Full solid angle* $= 4\pi.$

*Hence, the efficiency of the bulb is equal to* $\dfrac{2\pi}{3} : (4\pi) = \dfrac{1}{6}.$

*Thus, a sixth of the output lumens were used to illuminate the field, that is,* $100/6 \approx 16.7$ *(W).*

"OK", we said, and then we asked, "Isn't there a simpler solution?" The professor thought for a moment and produced the following result:

*Imagine that the playground reclines on the surface of a sphere, and in the center of this sphere is the light. It is easy to calculate what the radius of this sphere is*

$$R = \frac{a\sqrt3}{2}.$$

*Calculate the volume of the spherical sector on which a pyramid is inscribed:*

$$V = \frac{2}{3}\pi \bullet R^2 \bullet h = \frac{2}{3}\pi \bullet \left(\frac{a\sqrt3}{2}\right)^2 \bullet \left(\frac{a\sqrt3}{2} - \frac{a}{2}\right) = \frac{2}{3}\pi \bullet \frac{3a^2}{4} \bullet \frac{a \bullet (\sqrt3 - 1)}{2} =$$

$$= \frac{1}{4}\pi \bullet a^3 \bullet \left(\sqrt3 - 1\right)$$

*The volume of a sphere is equal* $V_{SP} = \dfrac{4}{3}\pi \bullet R^3 = \dfrac{4}{3}\pi \bullet \dfrac{a^3 \bullet 3\sqrt3}{8} = \pi \bullet \dfrac{a^3 \bullet \sqrt3}{2}.$

*Thus, the ratio of the volume of the sector is equal to the volume of the sphere:*

$$\frac{V}{V_{SP}} = \frac{2 \bullet (\sqrt3 - 1)}{4 \bullet \sqrt3} \approx \frac{1}{5}.$$

Indeed, in comparison this solution is much more streamlined and elegant. Let's suppose the answer is uncertain (as happens with most practical problems), then this is the better solution. But why didn't the professor propose this solution in the first place?

The thing is that people often rush into battle without stopping to seek out the optimal solution. People who have mastered a relatively narrow area of expertise are especially prone to act in this manner. But in life, it makes much more sense to develop the habit of figuring out the best route to the solution for any given task.

By the way, the problem of "TheLight above the Playground" has a solution:

*The lamp hangs exactly in the middle of the cube, with one side made up by the play-ground. The cube has 6 planes, and so the playground gets exactly 1/6 of the illumina-tion from the bulb.* $100/6 \approx 16.7$ *(W).*

This bird can no longer fly...

Indeed, is this not a more elegant solution? To find it, you had to pay attention to the conditions of this particular problem, to see its singularity. Such is the case both in science and in life: an intricate problem can be solved in general terms, but you can find loopholes and clues in the specific conditions that make the problem much easier to solve. These "nuggets" are natural conjectures to creative people.

At this point, we can suggest a productivity formula for creative thinking:

$$R = P_c \cdot P_m \cdot P_{kn} \cdot (1 + T) \cdot (1 + M),$$

where:

R is the result of mental activity, and its product;

$P_c$ is personal (innate) ability;

$P_m$ is the motivation to obtain results;

$P_{kn}$ is personal knowledge;

T represents the standard tools possessed by people in the areas of knowledge required for the results. For example, if the result of mental activity is a business plan, one of the standard tools is the ability to calculate interest;

M is the methods for finding new ideas that are generated from individual experience and/or purposefully studied. Examples of well-known methods include brainstorming, the method of focal objects, and TRIZ (the Theory of Inventive Problem Solving).

This formula strongly suggests that what schooling should be focused on is significantly improving the creative abilities of people. At school, children must be provided with experience in solving creative problems from a wide range of disciplines. As a result of this experience, they themselves will understand the value of knowledge, skills and techniques. This type of approach to learning corresponds much more closely with human nature than the current practice of endlessly filling the child with knowledge which he or she perceives to be of questionable value.

There is a common belief that first you need to give your child a solid base of knowledge, and then you can teach creative work. Some of our opponents believe that creative thinking skills should not be introduced until an individual enters college. It's kind of like you first need to fatten up the bird in the cage, and only then teach it to fly...

The acquisition itself, the process of harnessing knowledge should be creative, and that's when it will inspire, rather than discourage the student. And we believe that open problems are the primary component of this creative process.

A good education seeks to give a person the potential to be useful, needed, to live in harmony with others and with the surrounding world. But this world is full of contradictions, which turn into problems or obstacles on the path of life. Instead, they could be problems with solutions.

*A cow grazing on a hill...*

A fundamental contradiction
of mass education:
Each student is an individual
and has interests of his or her own;
but for the classroom to work,
the entire body of students
must be engrossed
in the subject at hand

**How to engage the students, or another case from the pedagogical practice of A. Guin.**

I was pondering how I would conduct a lesson on "electrostatic induction". I vividly imagined the class. Here are 30 teens of both sexes sitting in one room. Peter is thinking about Maria. Maria is thinking about Sergey. Sergey probably wants one thing only – and that is to avoid being called on. Who among them is thinking about electrostatic induction? No one! And who is it that asked me about it? No one! And now there I go walking into the classroom and writing the topic on the board. Is there anyone who will be inspired by this? No one ...

And this made me sad, and I began to think up a way out of this situation. How could I "fire up" the students over this topic? And what do I myself find interesting about induction? And then I came up with something...

"Hello, Class! I'll tell you a story taken right from life. I got it from the newspaper and it took place not far from our city. Imagine a pretty high hill with a grazing cow. The weather is rainy, and above the hill we see clouds, lightning, and thunder. And suddenly, after a lightning strike the cow drops dead. How did the cow die? What happened?"

After some discussion, the children come up with hypotheses:

- Lightning hit the cow;

- Lightning hit a puddle next to the cow, and an electric current killed her;

- The cow died of fear;

- The cow slipped and fell;

- The cow died of old age, and the lightning was just a coincidence;

- The lightning struck a tree, the tree fell and crushed the cow...

The first 7–8 hypotheses were generated quickly, another 2–3 students struggled to come up with something. I interrupt them:

"Sorry, class, no one has come across the real cause of death for that cow".

I see the surprise on their faces – well, what really happened? Now Peter, Maria, and Sergey, as well as everyone else are focused on only one thing: how is the death of the cow associated with lightning?

I announce the topic of the lesson: "Electrostatic induction".

I'll spend the next 10 minutes explaining the gist of this phenomenon. Let's see who can guess how it relates to our problem! Let's get started...

Now the attention of the class is focused on the topic of electrostatic induction.


**The Contradiction of Mass Education**

Every child and each student sitting in class is preoccupied with his or her life. Each one of them at any given moment in time is thinking about the things that matter to him, to her. But teachers are traditionally taught that this is not something that we should factor into how we teach. Yes, we try different ways to get the students to "tune in" at the beginning of the lesson, using oral questioning, or by going over the homework, or other standard methods from the arsenal of pedagogical techniques. But this is clearly not enough to get the students to actively participate in the lesson. For this, there is only one answer, and that is to awaken their interest. Open problems are particularly suited to this.


**When are open problems particularly good?**

Even if a traditional teacher introduces only 5–6 open problems on the subject over the course of the year, this alone can accomplish a lot. This is because the children will see and sense another way to experience the learning process; they will be given a taste of creative work in the lesson.

Curiousity and genuine interest in the world around you awakens your soul, opens your eyes and ears.

Open problems are good:

- For introducing a new topic.

- As a way to link one topic of instruction to another, one school subject to another, a way of illustrating the relationship of phenomena in nature. Here is an example of a problem that combines biology, physiology, and history.

### The Mysterious Power[27]

*For a long time scientists have sought answers to the question of what force transforms one substance into another: milk into cheese, fermented barley into beer, grape juice into wine and dough into bread. In the middle of the 18th century, the French scientist René Antoine Ferchault de Réaumur arrived at the notion that a search for a mysterious transforming power should be conducted in those places where it is most obviously manifested, i.e., where food is transformed in the body. The predominant view in his day was that the food in the stomach was simply mechanically crushed. The resulting small food particles were then simply mixed with gastric juice. Réaumur began to have doubts about this. And he decided to prove that in addition to whatever mechanism was activated in the stomach, there was also some kind of force processing the food.*
*What kind of experiment can be devised to prove that the way the stomach processes food is not merely mechanical?*

- How intriguing when a problem is given at the end of the lesson to launch a new topic. For example, what if in your plan for the next chemistry lesson the children are supposed to study the properties of acids? Before the lesson you give them a homework assignment:

### A violation of Archimedes' principle?

*According to Archimedes' principle, any body not in equilibrium in liquid will either float or sink. There is no other option. However, there is a liquid which, if you put an ordinary chicken egg into it, an amazing thing happens: the egg will alternate between floating and sinking.*
*What's going on here, and what kind of liquid is this?*

And if you also demonstrate this wonderful phenomenon, the interest will be extraordinary. In the next lesson, explain to the children why the egg behaves that way in a weak solution of hydrochloric acid. Moreover, this problem will give you the opportunity to naturally repeat Archimedes' principle, like a bridge linking physics and chemistry.

- It is also a great homework assignment in that it encourages the students to explore the subject, and also checks their understanding of the material being covered.

### Lightning: risk factors

*Lighting striking a person isn't really that unusual. Some people die, others – survive.*
*What factors make a lightning strike more lethal, and what factors mitigate the danger to human life?*
*In which case you are more likely to survive: when your clothes are wet, or when they're dry?*

This problem works well in a physics lesson subsequent to a study of "Electrical Discharges," or in a lesson on safety. Those who really understand the topic will be able to discuss it.

- As a creative homework assignment, it is a good overview of material that has already been covered or a way of casting new light on it.

---

[27] This problem was provided by TRIZ specialist Irina Andrjeevskaya.

# **W**ho is Creative Teacher?

## Creative Teachers:

Never stop developing;

Ask when they don't know something because they don't need to pretend that they know everything;

Back up their opinions with reasoning rather than authoritative dictates that alienate students;

Use open questions, open tasks, and tasks based dialog;

Freely share their creative skills!

**Alien Atmosphere**

*Some birds are excellent divers, and some fish, in contrast, leap into the air.*
*Find as many examples of animals who from time to time take excursions outside of their usual habitat. Analyze the reasons why this may occur. Think up a fantastic animal that lives in different environments.*

This problem involves a search for more information. It can form the basis of a small research project for students.

In preparing older students for Olympiads we developed the rule of 70–20–10. The rule is approximate, but this makes it no less useful. Approximately 70% of the problems given to the children are selected to be clearly manageable for them. This is to test their problem-solving skills and build their confidence in their own abilities. About 20% of the tasks given to the students push the limits of what they are able to solve. And about 10% are outside their range of actual knowledge and abilities. Their function is to push the child beyond his limits, and ensure he isn't overly confident. In the end, these really hard problems promote self-assessment skills, and increase self-confidence: the acquisition of new knowledge, working in teams, hints supplied by a more qualified person, or simply an intensive "battle" with the problem will sooner or later, lead to victory.

An interesting point: the value of the process of solving open problems does not have much to do with the result.[28] It really isn't that important if the children end up with the right answer or a passable answer to any given problem, or even if they never find a solution. Just as physical strength increases when you work out regularly doing your push-ups or punching a bag,[29] in the same way your creative strength grows when you try for a "breakthrough" on a problem that resists your best efforts. As a bonus, you'll witness the delight produced by a beautiful solution, respect for the scientists and inventors who first managed to come up with it, and appreciation of this demonstration of the complexity of the surrounding world.

## Differences between traditional and open problems

At workshops with teachers from various countries we would assign tasks which they were to work on in teams of five people:

1.  Examine the conditions in 25 problems;

2.  Select (for each team) a favorite problem;

3.  Justify the choice;

4.  Make a list of the differences between open problems and traditional approaches used in the schools.

What was interesting is that, regardless of the region, the resulting lists of characteristics for open problems were virtually identical. In general, these were as follows:

•      There is no clear algorithm for solving open problems — that is, there is no sequence of actions that is guaranteed (given proper execution) to lead to the correct result.

•      As a rule, the problems describe real-life situations.

•      There aren't any concrete conditions in open problems — that is, the problem statement contains additional information that may or may not pertain to the solution. The conditions may lack essential information, which must then be found in an accessible information space.

•      One problem can have many possible answers.

•      The question in an open problem might also be amorphous, obscure.

---

[28] Of course, it is given that the majority of the problems are nevertheless doable. Otherwise, you might inculcate a "loser's complex" in some of the children.

[29] This type of exercise is called static. They are considered to be very effective in developing physical strength.

The teacher, too, grows by working
with open problems

- The main objective of solving open problems is not to obtain an answer; rather, it is to develop thinking.
- There is no clear age grouping for open problems: children and adults alike are intrigued by them. Many problems can be solved both at the elementary school level and by adults
- The solution to the problem often triggers further investigation, a search for information on the topic.
- An open problem, solved by a team, makes it possible for many students, rather than just one, to share in the success.
- Open problems more often than not don't lie within the realm of a single academic subject — they are meta-disciplinary.
- Even a wrong answer can be interesting.
- Solving an open problem can be something like playing a game.
- You can continue to solve an open problem even if the sought-after answer has already been found.
- Open problems help you create both a competitive atmosphere and an atmosphere of cooperation (when working in teams).
- When the solutions to these problems are presented, students learn how to listen carefully and respond to the points made by other children.
- The process of solving open problems develops both imagination and intuition.
- You can select open problems for each school subject.
- The discussion and criticism of solutions to open problems develop critical thinking and encourages experimentation. This is a welcome contrast to simply hearing what the answer is.
- When students solve open problems, they learn to pay attention to the conditions of the problem because, after all, an answer/hint may be buried in the problem itself.
- Open problems stimulate discussions of solutions outside the confines of school, and draw in the student's parents and friends.
- Some of these problems are not just "pedagogical", they're truly developmental, teaching not just "what", but also "how" and "why".

We can personally testify to how working with open problems also leads to growth in the teacher. This is because an open problem generates the backdrop to life, itself, with all its unexpected twists. The teacher enters into free dialogue with the children, and she should be ready to improvise. And for this, she will be rewarded by the interest and recognition of her students.

The reasons for success
are much less discernable
to the public than are
the causes of failures

What determines the personal success rate[30] of the individual in life? We raised this question as an open research problem in a seminar with professors of law. We put on the board more then 20 of the "ultimate" factors for success. And we launched a discussion, in which we recalled historical and everyday examples, and constructed a hierarchy of potential success factors...

•    Money? Availability of start-up funds?

Where there has been an elegant idea and an ability to solve problems, there are plenty of examples where huge capital was created when funds were limited.

> *Wozniak sold his premium XII-65 calculator for $500. Jobs sold his Volkswagen van to secure half of the profit from the enterprise.[31] This is how he produced the initial capital for the company Apple – one of the leading players in the market for computers.*

The shipping magnate Aristotle Onassis, financial king Mayer Amschel Rothschild, oil tycoon John D. Rockefeller, British paleoanthropologist Mary Leakey, originator of the first mass-produced car Henry Ford — they were all innovators, inventors, solvers of open problems.

At the same time, history is replete with examples of a different order, when a person loses everything due to an unfortunate decision...

•    School and higher education?

We all know that the best students in school are not always the most successful in life. Even in science, scholastic success, the amount of knowledge acquired in school is not a determining factor for success.

> *Asaph Hall did not receive any formal training in astronomy and came to astronomy not from another field of knowledge, but from a realm far removed from science in general. Asaph was a carpenter. Having studied under the guidance of his wife, a math teacher, he soon displayed such success that he was invited to visit American observatories. In 1877 Hall immortalized his name with his discovery of the moons of Mars — Phobos and Deimos.*
>
> *Being a fairly well-known American artist, but with no comprehension of anything in a field that was totally alien to him – the theory of electricity, Morse became interested in the notion of data transmission over wires at the age of 42. He subsequently invented the telegraph, and became one of the founders and the first president of the National Academy in New York.*

•    What about health?

Of course. But here, too, there are many exceptions.

> *You can see the background he had to overcome by the letter Vasili Eroshenko, the son of a peasant, received from his father. The address was as follows: "China, Peking Pekin University Prokhfesor of Ispiranto Vasili Eroshenko From his origins as a blind peasant lad, Eroshenko managed to secure his place in higher education in a variety of disciplines, and he worked as a professor of Esperanto not only in Beijing, but also at the University of Tokyo.*
>
> *Eroshenko's output was enormous: Three collections of novellas and stories in Japanese. Now the writer Ero-san (the name by which Eroshenko is known in Japan) has entered the canon of Japanese literature, and his tales are required reading in Japanese schools. In China, he is known as the writer and playwright Ayrosyanke. He was the first in the world to popularize writings from Siamese and Burmese folklore.*

---

[30] We have defined the concept of "success" as follows: a person is successful if he considers himself a success and if the people around him concur with this assessment. In other words, if in his life he has achieved something significant for himself and for others.

[31] Facts from J. Mingo. Sekreti uspekha velikikh kompanii (52 istorii iz biznesa i torgovli)[Success Secrets of Great Companies (52 Stories from Business and Trade)]. SPb., 1995.

School for
Creative
Thinkers

Your life itself is an open problem, indeed.
Solve it, and surely you will succeed!

*His newspaper articles in English, German and Esperanto have been preserved. Blind children in Turkmenistan still use his alphabet in school — he developed braille for the Turkmen language (his braille script for the Chukchi was not completed). He developed a unique method of teaching foreign languages, and a method for teaching the blind how to move about independently. Eroshenko himself walked about without a stick, even in unfamiliar cities. The fact that he was blind was not notable until one was close by.[32]*

*Stephen Hawking is known throughout the world as an English cosmologist, a man of genius. He has long served as a professor at Cambridge University. Born in 1942, while still a young man he was diagnosed with a form of the rare motor neuron affliction known as Lou Gehrig's disease, in which a person loses mobility. All he can move are the facial muscles in one cheek. He controls the muscles in this cheek to interface with a sensor mounted in a camera on his desk. This is how the physicist operates his computer and communicates with others via an electronic voice synthesizer.*

It seems that there is only one quality that is absolutely and indubitably indispensable for achieving significant success: the ability to solve problems. Of course, we are talking about open problems – professional, domestic, psychological...

The creative person sees open problems all around her. She sees them where others see misfortune or an unsolvable problem ... You just learn to open your eyes, and then the world will present itself as an infinite open problem in which the physicist discerns specific problems of his own, the biologist, too, sees specific problems related to her field, and the teacher, as well. We must learn to see problems the same way that the blind Eroshenko could see them. Here, by the way, is an example of a pedagogical problem with an astonishingly beautiful solution from Eroshenko:

*While seeking out Turkmen school students (he also did this by himself) Eroshenko came across a blind orphan named Durdy. It's amazing how this kid even survived. At six years of age, all he had known was hunger and constant beating from begging on the streets. He lived under the religious conviction that all people are beasts, and that he himself was not needed in this world. Eroshenko brought him to school, fed him, and gave him water. The standard approach in educational circles in such cases is to gradually win the trust of the child over the course of several years. But Eroshenko didn't want to wait for this to happen. He led Durdy to the mountains (by the way, Eroshenko wasn't a bad amateur mountain climber). Together they approached the edge of a cliff, and Eroshenko asked the kid to shout his name. "I am Durdy!" he shouted. And the echo repeated his name several times. "You see", said Eroshenko, "even here in the mountains, you are known and loved..."*

*Many years after the death of Eroshenko, Durdy Pitkulaev served as the director of the school in Turkmenistan.[33]*

Born in Greece, the international businessman Aristotle Onassis, and the blind Russian, Vasily Eroshenko — what do they have in common? The men themselves are different, as were their circumstances and the times in which they lived, yet both were successful. One of them might have remained a night dispatcher at a US port, and the other –- a poor peasant in a Russian village. But they knew how to see problems, and rather than fearing them, they solved them. For them, just like breathing, solving problems was a natural process.

History is rife with cases of people who, after inventing something of great use to humankind, nevertheless die in poverty with no public recognition. The fact is that the implementation of an invention is itself an invention. It is not always the person who came up with the invention or discovery who can successfully introduce it to the world, who can motivate the people around them and inspire them.

*How can you demonstrate that bent furniture legs are just as reliable as straight legs? When faced with potential investors, one designer threw the chair out of the sixth-floor window. The chair fell on the grass, trembling, and like an arrow, balanced on the grass on one leg. Did it work? Clearly, he had made his point.[34]*

[32] From the article: I. Murashkovsky, Yu. Murashkovsky "Ya zazheg v svoem serdtse ogon... " [I lit a fire in my heart] http://www.trizway.com/art/creative/77.html

[33] From the article: I. Murashkovsky, Yu. Murashkovsky "Ya zazheg v svoem serdtse ogon... " [I lit a fire in my heart] http://www.trizway.com/art/creative/77.html

[34] From the archives of Victor Timokhov, TRIZ master.

The main objective of the new pedagogy
is to operate at the frontiers of knowledge,
in unusual situations,
to solve open problems

In order for the Creative Personality to succeed, it is vital that she possess the ability to solve problems outside of the profession, beyond the narrow branch of science or technology. It has always been this way. Remember the puzzle of the "Golden Fire" about the peasant who first built and then burnt the house at the fair and made a fortune as a result? Here is the prepared answer to why he did this:

> *The peasant had invented a fire retardant. The wood, which he had saturated with the retardant, was nonflammable. He built a house and set fire to it at the industrial exhibit at the fair, thus creating the perfect advertisement of his invention. Along the way, he also collected some funds from skeptics who had bet against him.*[35]

People such as this are "universal problem solvers", and they are essential to humankind as a whole and each country in particular.

Entirely new problems are emerging with different attributes that require people to quickly process poorly organized information, systematically assess complex situations and the consequences of decisions, and to make unconventional decisions. Accordingly, there are also new professions. For example, risk managers, or, more precisely, risk-advisers, i.e., consultants for unusual situations, or specialists in the management of major man-made disasters. But most importantly, in today's world, components of creative thinking, such as independence and the ability to think critically, the ability to understand poorly structured information, a positive attitude towards change – these are attributes that all of us need. A society in which people who lack this are a minority will resist objective changes, hinder progress, and such a society is easily manipulated. In the end, this society will experience stunted development.

> *A study by Wellcome Trust found that graduates of schools in England are not prepared to deal with complex ethical issues generated by modern science. Almost nothing is being done to teach students to think rationally about problems such as embryonic human cloning, animal testing and genetically modified foods. Students develop opinions that are outside the realm of science. Teachers are concerned about low interest in important events and news in general. They also note that students have very strong opinions on issues such as the animal rights and cloning, but that these are based on scant evidence.*[36]

The scientific and technical problems facing us are not getting any easier. And as long as we live on earth, we will be confronted with ecological problems. Even as we continue developing our scientific capabilities, we must be aware of the risks and what they entail.

The fact is, we make mistakes, and the more power we have, the costlier are those mistakes. Ships go down, oil spills into the waters, forests burn to the ground, wars break out... These events result in huge costs. The further we progress, the more our approach to the open problems around us matter, and the more they become a determining factor in the quality of life throughout society.

Yesterday's pedagogical industry was targeted at raising a person to conscientiously carry out well-established functions, and this, in turn, has outlived its own function. Of course, it is still fighting for survival through the introduction of non-essential changes, cajoling us and diverting us from the real issue. The main goal of education for a new era is to each people to operate at the frontiers of knowledge, in unusual situations, to solve open problems.

---

[35] Grani tvorchestva [The Verge of Creativity] / Comp. B.S. Weinberg. Sverdlovsk, 1989.
[36] Source of information: http://www.rusbiotech.ru/2003/old/arch_n_7.html

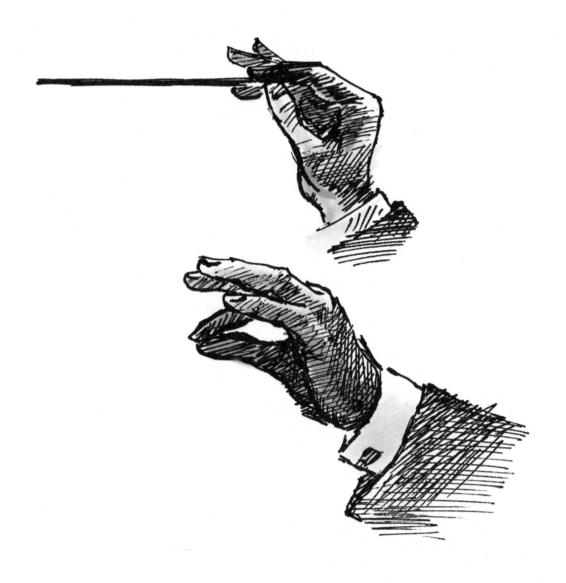

…We can increase the overall level of creativity. There is no contradiction
whatsoever between "talent" and "education".
Each coach or singing teacher will confirm this..

Edward de Bono,
a British psychologist and author, and expert
in the field of creative thinking

## ANSWERS TO FREQUENTLY ASKED QUESTIONS

In over a quarter of a century of professional work in TRIZ, the authors have conducted more than 200 seminars in different countries – from one-day workshops to two-week courses of study. At each seminar people submit questions. Some of these questions are often submitted by different audiences – these are the most popular questions and answers.

### What kind of people do you call creative? What is creativity?

Creativity is ingenuity. A creative person is an innovative individual. That is, a person with the potential to create something new and useful both for society as a whole, and for herself.

There is a common misconception that creativity is the ability to speak eloquently on any topic, get out of any situation, and so forth. In fact, while these also indicate creativity, they are clearly insufficient and not fundamental. Another misconception: Creativity is the antithesis of discipline. Of course, training a creative person for slavish, wretched, inefficient work is hard – everything in the creative individual will protest against such work. But the study of biographies of great creative personalities convinces us that these were people with a very high level of discipline – they possessed self-discipline. If such a person is engaged in proper work corresponding to his understanding, then he will move mountains, and there will be no need to monitor what he does. Another important note: Creativity is always accompanied by criticality and self-criticism. Armed with a critical attitude toward the surrounding world, the creative personality identifies deficiencies and turns them into open problems. Her propensity toward self-criticism will compel her to carry out painstaking work, safeguarding her from letting raw or useless ideas emerge on top.

### Does every single person have to be creative? Not everyone can be an inventor...

In today's world, our respective destinies are dictated by how creative we are. In the end, the primary invention of each one of us is the life we create for ourselves. For just one of many indications of this, you need only look at websites for job-hunters. The best companies are looking for creative people...

> *"Microsoft seeks employees who can outline multiple options for solutions to complex problems, and then rationally select the best".*[37]

### Is it generally possible to learn how to be creative? They say that this is an innate talent that you're either born with or not...

Teaching creative thinking can be easily compared to other types of learning activities: swimming, playing the violin or chess. In all these cases, there are two equally important components to the teaching process: the game rules and practice. To some degree practice is of greater importance. You can talk as much as you want about the movements involved in swimming, but until the athlete drills these movements into her very muscles, you won't make a swimmer out of her. This also applies to playing the violin or chess. On the other hand, persistent and successful practice could lead to a person becoming a master at a particular endeavor, even without any knowledge of the rules. Or, it would seem the rules don't play a role, because they are not verbalized during training, although they are inherent. Indeed, rules that are well-taught and accompanied by practice drastically reduce the time to master the task, to achieve greater success, to increase the number of those who move from novice to master.

The rest will be clear from the following example:

> *Neuroscientists Steven Quartz and Terrence Sejnowski report: "If you're born with certain characteristics, this doesn't mean that you'll remain that way forever ... Your experience of interacting with the world changes the structure of your brain, chemical processes, and gene expression; often these profound changes are taking place throughout your life".*[38]

---

37 Career Insider Career, №5, 10/09/2007. Supplement to the newspaper Elite Personnel.

38 From the book: J. Eykaff Nachni (Vrezh' strahu po licu, perestan' byt' "normal'nym" i zajmis' chem-to stojashhim) [Start (Whop fear in the face, stop being "normal" and go do something worthwhile)]. Moscow: 2014

Would you like to know
what kind of standard of living
the next generation is likely to enjoy?
This will correspond
to the level of education
we provide the children of today.

### At what age should we nurture creativity?

We have met in life adults who seemed completely "ill-equipped" for creativity. We believe that, in effect, this is first and foremost the results of traditional education and training. Support for innate creativity should begin at birth. The skills associated with creative thinking can be targeted and developed in the family at a very early age, and at school – from kindergarten. There are many tried and tested tools to develop these skills. It is important that from an early age the child experiences a wide array of successful creative endeavors.

As adults, almost all of us can also develop our creative skills. It's like learning to play a musical instrument. There are people who learn guitar or piano as adults, and quite successfully – although virtuosos usually are those who have trained from childhood.

### I have a child enrolled in a good school. Almost all its graduates enter good universities. How can I tell if this school devotes attention to the development of creative skills?

With rare exception, traditional educational institutions largely "dampen" natural creativity, rather than develop it. Although in fairness it must be said that the exceptions are increasing in number.

Most schools focus on having children memorize data, but do not stimulate the development of thinking. However, if your child is given the opportunity to attain self-actualization in the school thanks to his intellectual creativity, has freedom of choice within the scope of the subject, is able to freely express himself, and if he appreciates your and other people's opinions, shares with you his thoughts and new interesting problems, then he is lucky to be enrolled in an exceptional school, and you are also in luck.

### Given existent conditions and the current educational climate, can a new system of education based on developing thinking really be constructed?

Yes. If we're talking about the public education system, it will still take place to some extent, but extremely slowly and inefficiently. This is because there are far too many people involved in the system, and too much inertia has built up to make effective changes. However, there are ways to make modern education really modern in substance relatively quickly. We believe that in 5–7 years we can largely rebuild the education system, increase its effectiveness. Of course, this depends on political will and resources.

After all, you're not surprised that to reach a championship level in sports you have to maintain your training, are you? So it is with the mind. What do you want to achieve? Practice!

- How does one select problems for each topic being addressed?
- How can we assess the children's ideas for solving open problems?
- Are there typical scenarios for lessons promoting creative skills?

We provide answers at our seminars and workshops to questions like these, and also to many other questions pertaining to how to implement open problems in your teaching practice. We conduct training sessions on solving problems, teach teachers to design their own open problems, develop lesson plans.

## ABOUT THE SCHOOL FOR CREATIVE THINKERS PROJECT

More than a quarter of a century ago we began the first experiments on adapting the theory of inventive problem solving — TRIZ — to the education process.

Over the years a certain understanding of the new curriculum took shape along with the corresponding learning technologies. There are special exercises to develop different creative skills and compilations of educational open problems on various topics. In 2000, a group of TRIZ specialists and teachers and enthusiasts came together in the social Universal Solver Laboratory A few years later the Laboratory came to be called Education for a New Era. By 2010, the Laboratory and its members began operating in different countries, and subsequently evolved into the international public association also called Education for a New Era. A vast body of experience has since been accumulated, numerous books have been published, and more than 300 informational and training seminars and workshops have been held around the world.

In 2011, we launched the School for Creative Thinkers. The project has evolved into a modular program for creative skills, orienting children and adolescents toward self-improvement, honing their perceptional abilitties, and helping them embrace a creative life. The program includes training in how to work in a creative group, developing the habit of considering facts from different points of view, seeking out and making decisions, calculating the long-term consequences of decision, seeing the non-obvious, and more.

Several books published as part of the School for Creative Thinkers project have been translated and published in the United States, France, Japan, China, South Korea, Malaysia, Poland, the Czech Republic and other countries. VITA-PRESS Publishers is our strategic partner for publications. Operations in the Russian Federation carried out by the Center for Modern Educational Technologies (TSSTO), Moscow; LLC TRIZ-profi and other partners; in the US — by the enterprise Education for a New Era.

To locate our primary Russian site, simply type "Education for a New Era" into any search engine. The site features a monthly newsletter: announcements, news, updates, and articles on methodology, presentations, debates, information on books and how to purchase them through online retailers. Our English language site is under continual development. You may find it at www.enecenter.com.

We believe that as our children develop the ability to solve problems — both their own and problems of a global nature — the world will become a better place...

If you are interested in this project, you can register on the website Education for a New Era. If you have any suggestions for participation in the project — contact us at lot@trizway.com in Russian or at mgbarkan@enecenter.com in English.

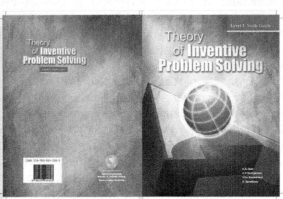

These books all aim to teach people
how to negotiate their way
through open problems.

**AN ANNOTATED LIST OF BOOKS**

### G. Altov
### AND SUDDENLY THE INVENTOR APPEARED

Published in Russia and the U.S.

This entertaining book served as the source material for a column in the newspaper Pionerskaya pravda.

"Invent? That's so hard! That's so simple!", written by Genrich Altshuller under the pseudonym G. Altov. Genrich Altshuller is the founder of TRIZ (Theory of Inventive Problem Solving).

It's a lengthy process to raise someone as an inventor, and therefore it's important to begin as soon as possible. And while grade school does not introduce the theory and methodology of technical innovation, this book helps you take the first steps on your own toward this.

The learning objectives in the book are derived from actual technical solutions, officially recognized inventions. These inventions are cited only as "controlled responses," used to suggest the variety of solutions, any one of which could be successfully employed. The problems outlined in the book do not require any special knowledge. Thus, the knowledge required for their solution is found in most school curricula. Altogether, the educational problems in the book serve as a bridge over the chasm from simply solving technological problems to thinking like an inventor.

### Altshuller G.S.
### TO FIND AN IDEA: INTRODUCTION TO THE THEORY OF CREATIVE PROBLEM SOLVING

Published in Russia, USA, Japan, China, Malaysia, and Estonia.

Many have attempted to comprehend the mystery of creativity, but Genrich Saulovich Altshuller is the only one who succeeded in creating a theory of inventive problem solving – TRIZ. Altshuller discovered the basic laws of inventiveness and demonstrated how we control the process of creating inventions. This process requires organizing one's thinking, overcoming psychological inertia, working toward an ideal solution, and resolving the contradictions hidden in non-standard tasks. TRIZ is recognized throughout the world as a teaching methodology and is also used for solving creative problems in many areas of human activity, ranging from construction and design to advertising, public relations, and management. This edition features the basic tools provided in classical TRIZ. There are also numerous examples of inventions created using TRIZ methods, and problems for independent study.

### Guin A.A., Kudryavtsev, A.V., Bubentsov, V.Yu., Seredinsky A.
### THE THEORY OF INVENTIVE PROBLEEM SOLVING (a study guide for certification on Level I of MATRIZ certification system)

Published in Russia, the USA, Japan, China, Malaysia, and Estonia.

A TRIZ study guide written by a group of authors with years of experience as consultants on solving non-standard tasks and teaching for various audiences: businessmen, engineers, university professors, scientists and students. The book is written in an accessible language with a clean layout, and is easily navigated. From reviews of TRIZ Masters, the author of 150 inventions, Samsung consultant Gennady Ivanov:

> *"You hold in your hands a book that, if you so wish it, can change your life, and make it more interesting, meaningful and successful. The materials in this guide are your first step toward managed creativity".*

**A.A. GUIN**
**TECHNIQUES IN EDUCATIONAL TECHNOLOGY:**
**FREEDOM OF CHOICE. OPENESS. ACTIVITIES. FEEDBACK. IDEALITY**
Published in Russia, Belarus, Ukraine, Poland.[39]

This book on methodology is a bestseller among teachers. Its target readers are practicing teachers, and methodologists regardless of subject specialization. It contains tested and clearly formulated techniques to increase productivity in the classroom. These are classroom management techniques: how to maintain discipline and focus, implement non-traditional forms of work in the classroom, and bring about student collaboration and effective testing. Classroom tactics: how to interest students in lectures, repeat basic materials, sustain interest in problems, and teach literary language. The book also provides techniques for teachers on how to organize their work.

The structure of the book is streamlined and to the point The teacher is initiated in solutions to fundamental educational issues: how to teach children without initiating damaging competivenes. The author suggests that every teacher can set the stage for his or her own teaching practice by selecting the sequence of techniques that best suits one's individual teaching style.

**A.A. Guin**
**Smart Tales from Brainy the Cat**
Published in Russia, USA, France, China, South Korea, Malaysia, Poland, and the Czech Republic.

This gift book for children of elementary school age is richly illustrated. It features a collection of real inventive tasks. Of course, it's like a fantastic storybook for young children It contains 36 entertaining problems. At the center of each of them is a fabulous hero who must find a way out of a predicament. Along with the hero, the young reader looks for a way out of each situation, and is aided by a series of tips and suggestions. This book is a great way to develop a child's attention span, teach him how to see hidden information, liberate his imagination, and discern what is important. Help your child develop creative thinking abilities in a positive psychological atmosphere.

Use this book to enliven activities for groups of children, for example, birthday parties for your son or daughter. Children love working together to solve problems. Organize games such as "What? Where? When?" The names of the tasks are in sealed in envelopes, and the children throw dice to find out what envelope they get.

If you are an elementary school teacher, then there's no need to wait for a holiday. This book gives you the materials for vivid, memorable lessons.

If the child already knows the answer from the book or cartoon? Well, fine. Firstly, let the child notice that her familiar fairy tales contain hidden problems. And secondly, let her try to find another way out of each fantastic situation. By the way, children often come up with solutions that are more interesting than those proposed in the original fairytale.

**A.A. Guin, A.A. Serebrennikov.**
**PLAYSCRIPTS FOR ELEMBENTARY SCHOOLS BASED ON FAIRYTALES**
This handbook presents 10 scenarios for mini-performances to be performed by children with the help of their teacher. At the heart of each of each script is an entertaining creative challenge from the book Smart Tales from Brainy the Cat. In the course of performances children become the "consultants" to the heroes of each fairytale, suggesting possible solutions to them, helping them out of difficult situations.

For each challenge, there are several possible solutions. The more tips the children give the heroes, meaning the more solutions they come up with, the more exciting the play is. Discussions about the best solutions and why they are the best choices can be woven into the fabric of the performance.

Interactive performances can be staged during extracurricular activities or for group activities in daycare. They can serve as an integral part of extracurricular education aimed at developing creative thinking.

---

39 Partial publication.

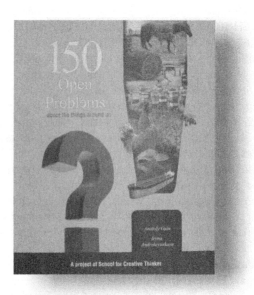

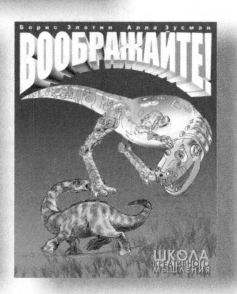

**A.A. Guin, I.Yu. Andrzheevskaya**
**150 CREATIVE PROBLEMS ABOUT THE THINGS AROUND US**
Published in Russia and Malaysia

This book contains 150 original problems. They cover interesting phenomena from vegetable and animal life and our surrounding natural world. All of the problems are unique. To solve them, the child must learn to think, to compare facts, analyze them, make assumptions and draw conclusions. Preparing for life in a rapidly changing world of information is a far more lucrative endeavor than cramming in unnecessary information. The book is designed to train students in creativity, i.e., to provide students in grade school and also high school with the skills associated with inventive and research thinking. The problems in the book range from the spheres of biology, ecology and rural life to approaches to solving open problems. The problems are accompanied by interesting historical information and rare facts from the plant and animal world.

- Why is it that moss grows only on the north side of trees?
- Why do ants like to "soak in the sun" in the spring atop their anthill?
- How do spiders move about their own webs without getting stuck?
- How can you get a worm out of a jar of soil when you're fishing without getting your hands dirty?
- Where do fish come from in a newly dug pond?
- Where is that hedgehogs taking that apple, and why?
- How does a cow turn hay into milk?

- These and similar questions can be shared with adolescents. And now we can help our kids learn how to negotiate the wealth of information sources available to them in their quest for answers.

**A.A. Guin, A.F. Kavtrev.**
**CREATIVITY BOWL: COMPETITION INSTRUCTIONS**

This handbook explains in detail what a "creativity bowl" is and how to conduct one in general educational institutions. Challenges for the participants of these competitions are provided, along with the criteria for assessing their solutions.

Today, creativity bowls are held for different age groups: from elementary school students to company teammates. Teams in different educational institutions can compete with each other, including online. Students in school can compete against their teachers or parents.

The book is written for teachers, methodologists, school administrators, and teachers engaged in extracurricular education.

**V. Zlotin, A. Zusman**
**JUST IMAGINE!**

Once upon a time in the USSR in the 80s of the last century, many of today's TRIZ teachers were making their first attempts to develop creative skills in children. They were guided by the remarkable book A Month Under the Stars of Fantasy. Authors, practicing inventors, students of TRIZ founder Genrich Altshuller, share their experiences working with children. They talk about how kids in schools are unable to acquire the quality that is most in demand for any profession – both then and now, it wasn't part of the curriculum. This quality is creative thinking, the ability to always and everywhere uncover new, innovative solutions.

And now, decades later, the authors of this book have updated it to include the current situation in education. Boris Zlotin and Alla Zusman are longterm residents of the United States. They occupy high positions, and are very busy people. But at the request of their students, they have volunteered the time to make new versions of this book. The book is available online under the title Just Imagine!. This edition of the book is a real gift for lovers of creativity in education.

### A.A. Guin, A.F. Kavtrev.
### EXPLAIN THE UNEXPLAINABLE

Published in Russia, South Korea.

The first book in the series "The World Library 2.0" is a fascinating read for those who are preparing themselves for a creative life. Creative (open) problems based on physics and technology are laid out in a light, entertaining style, accompanied by interesting background information, amazing facts, and commentary from scientists. To help the reader solve them, various questions and tasks are supplied, basic and supplemental information, hints and suggestions, to support and incentivize the reader in her quest for answers. The illustrations depict the mysterious phenomena of the world. All the problems included in the collection are original and are based on real events and facts.

### A.A. Guin, I.Yu. Andrzheevskaya
### ATTACK OF THE PREDATORS

Published in Russia, South Korea.

This is the second volume in the series "The World Library 2.0". It is a fascinating read for anyone who loves the unexpected and ingenious twists of thought.

Nature provides the puzzles, and people provide the solutions. An understanding of the laws of nature is a huge advantage in this. But the real understanding comes only from someone who knows how to apply knowledge in a non-standard situation, that is, to solve open problems, which proliferate in the natural world.

The inventions of living creatures in their struggle for survival are transformed by the authors into engaging challenges. In the course of responding to them, the reader can unleash his wit and creative imagination, and give free rein to his ability to think outside the box. The book provides recommendations to the solver that teach him or her to apply techniques from nature: The rule of sufficient ideality, the rule of resources, the rule of the conversion of harm into benefit, the rule of the repetition of successful finds, the rule of multiple solutions. The problems are accompanied by additional information which provides a more complete picture to the reader of living nature.

The book is written for inquisitive children and adults.

### A.A. Guin, I.Yu. Andrzheevskaya
### HOW NOT TO BECOME PREY

Published in Russia, South Korea.

This is the third volume in the series "The World Library 2.0". In this book, the reader is given 60 problems. We can assume that these were all problems once faced by animals, and what followed was a quest for a solution that, if none were found, could cost them their life. Those who could not solve the problem are now extinct. These are the inventions of living beings in the struggle for survival transformed into entertaining problems. These problems not only cover the student's understanding of the laws of nature, they also provide training in how to solve open problems. The problems are arranged by the degree of difficulty and are accompanied by tips, motivational phrases, interesting queries and additional tasks that are associated with each problem. If you admire nature and you love her marvelous innovations, this book is for you.

### S.A. Faer. V.I. Timokhov
### HALF MY KINGDOM FOR AN IDEA!

This is the fourth volume in the series "The Library World 2.0". Spanish grandees and the captive king of France, the Russian traveler Sundakov and French philosopher Michel de Montaigne, the ancient Greek hero Achilles and the Beatles are just some of the characters you meet in the pages of this book. All of them were in situations where, in order to survive or to emerge victorious from a situation, they had to use their heads. And they succeeded! The book contains 100 dire situations. They were used in the course "Development of the Creative Imagination" at a TRIZ training seminar. TRIZ is the Theory of Inventive Problem Solving.

Every person at least once in her life, and usually more often, finds herself in a situation where some creative ingenuity would really help out. Now you can prepare in advance for these situations!

The book is written for inquisitive children, adults parents, teachers, those who want to make their lessons more interesting, and teachers in extracurricular education.

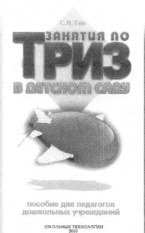

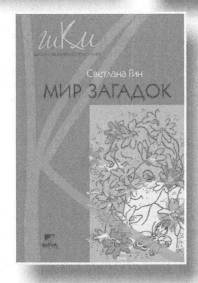

**S.I. Guin**
## TRIZ FOR KINDERGARTEN
Published in Russia and Belarus

The book provides educational activities for children in their fifth and sixth year of life from the arsenal of TRIZ pedagogy. These activities are targeted at developing speech and creativity in preschool children, as well as at enhancing the quality of their thought processes by inculcating flexibility, mobility, consistency, dialectical thinking, and activating inquisitiveness and the desire for innovation.

For preschool teachers.

**S.I. Guin**
## THE WORLD OF RIDDLES
This handbook is a detailed plan for developing lessons for the course "The World of Riddles", which introduces children to the world around them through solving and composing riddles. Children learn the properties of objects, develop their senses, acquire the skills for systemic and dialectical thinking, get acquainted with the concepts of the theory of inventive problem solving (TRIZ), and journey through the Land of Riddles.

The book is intended for grade school teachers.

**S.I. Guin**
## THE WORLD OF PEOPLE
Published in Russia and Belarus
A handbook for elementary school teachers.

Course content – a systemic examination of a person from different points of view: biological, anatomical, psychological, and social. A special feature of the course is the construction of the lessons in the form of a problematic dialogue with children, in which they are in an actively cognitive point of view. The object of study itself becomes the child herself at the age of 7–8 years.

The manual is a detailed plan for lesson development for a one-year course for the first (or second) year of primary school.

**S.I. Guin**
## THE WORLD OF FANTASY
Published in Russia and Belarus
A handbook for elementary school teachers.

The course "World of Fantasy" aims to teach children the skills of creative thinking and guided imagery. The methodological basis of the course is the development of techniques to foster creativity from the theory of inventive problem solving (TRIZ). The manual is a detailed lesson plan comprising 31 lessons for students in first and second grade, including recommendations for each lesson, sample dialogues, analysis of possible difficulties, and illustrative materials for each lesson.

**S.I. Guin**
## THE WORLD OF LOGIC
Published in Russia and Belarus
A handbook for elementary school teachers.

The course "World of Logic" aims to teach children creative thinking skills and guided imagery, compare, classify, give definitions, build inferences, highlight regularities, reason, and so on. The manual is a detailed lesson plan with 32 lessons for the final year of primary school. It includes recommendations for implementing each complete lesson or simply in stages, including sample dialogues, an analysis of possible difficulties in the classroom, and descriptions on how to overcome them.

**G.I. Ivanov**
**DENIS THE INVENTOR**
Published in Russian, U.S.A., Germany, South Korea, Ukraine.

This book is written for children by a Russian inventor, an expert on the Theory of Inventive Problem Solving (TRIZ). The book is designed to foster the development of the creative abilities of students in elementary school and junior high, and contains numerous illustrations.

Along with the hero of the book, young readers will take a fascinating journey into the world of creativity, and together they'll solve a host of interesting inventive problems. Readers will be convinced that everyone can learn to invent if they only wanted to, the innate propensity toward inventiveness in every boy and every girl that was given to them at birth. It is important that they retain these skills and develop them as much as possible. If you're raising an inquisitive, creative child then this book is for him or her.

A review from a reader:

> *"My son is reading it, and he's completely absorbed. Unfortunately, there aren't enough TRIZ books for children, but in this book everything is very accessible and fun. Now, my son keeps giving me inventive puzzles. A wonderful book, beautiful illustrations and the print quality is also high. The paper is white, glossy, and fine. Vivid pictures. I think I'll buy a few of these as gifts for friends".*
>
> *Marina Bogachyova*

**G.I. Ivanov**
**FORMULAS FOR CREATIVITY, OR HOW TO LEARN HOW TO INVENT**
Published in Russia, South Korea, Germany, China, Serbia.

This book is for anyone who wants to become an inventor, who is fascinated by the world of technical creativity, and wants a deeper understanding of it. The purpose of the book is to help young readers develop inventive abilities. The target audience is high school students.

The book presents the problems solved by members of the club of young inventors led by the author. The guys in the club knew they could improve the world — what's the big deal? Many of them have already created "adult", officially patented inventions.

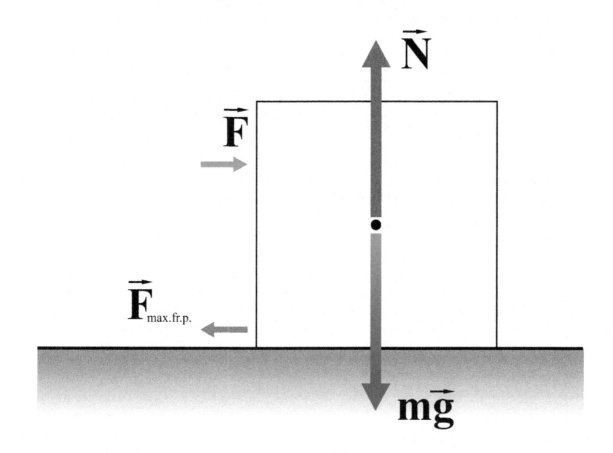

The force of the wind impact F and the force of friction
Fmax.fr.p.

## CALCULATION FOR "UNUSUAL STONES IN DEATH VALLEY"

Let us calculate the speed of the wind needed to move a stone located on a clay surface slick with rain. We first assess the size of the stones typically found on the surface of the dry lake bed in Death Valley. Assume for simplicity's sake that the stone is shaped like a cube. Let the value of the edge of the cube equal $a$. Then the volume of the stone, on the one hand, is:

$$V = a^3. (1)$$

On the other hand, the volume of the stone $V$ is related to its mass $m$ and density $\rho_k$ by the formula:

$$V = m / \rho_k. (2)$$

From formulas (1) and (2) we get:

$$a = \sqrt[3]{m / \rho_k}. (3)$$

Let us assess the size of the stone. According to the problem statement, the mass of the stones reaches $m \approx 300$ kg.

Based on reference data, we select an average stone density $\rho_k = 2500$ kg/m³. Thus, according to the calculation, we get $a \approx 0{,}5$ m, the stones may have a size of 0,5·0,5·0,5 m. This is a rather impressive size. No wonder the race car drivers are afraid of these stones.

We now assess the magnitude of the force $F$, parallel with the surface of the lake bottom, that is strong enough move the stone. This force $F$ should exceed the value of maximum friction force $F_{max.fr.p.}$, which can be calculated by the formula:

$$F_{max.fr.p.} = \mu N = \mu mg, (4)$$

where $\mu$ is the maximum coefficient of static friction, which in our estimation can be regarded as equal to the coefficient of sliding friction; and $N$ is the reaction forces. Since the stone is on a horizontal surface, then $N = mg$. For the assessment, we calculate $g = 10$ m/s².

What should be the coefficient of friction $\mu$ in this case? In the available references we couldn't find the frictional drag coefficient for a stone on wet clay. As we all know, it's extremely difficult to walk on wet clay. If you have experienced this kind of "fun", then you know that the "slipperiness" of wet clay is close to the "slipperiness" of ice.

So we took from the reference the coefficient for friction drag of steel on ice and just in case, we doubled the value. After all, the stone doesn't look much like ice skates. What we ended up with is $\mu = 0{,}03$. After plugging the data into the formula (4), we obtain: $F_{max.fr.p.} \approx 100$ N. Thus, the force $F$, which is required to move the stone, exceeds 100 N. It doesn't take too much force, really, to move a stone weighing 300 kg. But can the wind generate this kind of force?

The amount of force generated by air flow on an an obstacle can be calculated by the formula:

$$F = \rho_в S v^2, (5)$$

where $\rho_в$ is air density, $\rho_в = 1{,}2$ kg/m³; $S$ is the area of the face of the stone, $S = a^2$; $v$ is the air flow rate, i.e. in this case the wind speed.

The derivation of the formula (5) is shown below. Try to determine this formula yourself. The knowledge required for this doesn't go beyond what the level of a high school physics class.

It follows from (5) we obtain the formula for wind speed:

$$v = \sqrt{F / \rho_в S}. (6)$$

Substituting the data, we obtain wind speed $v \approx 20$ m/s. In the conditions for the problem it was noted that in Death Valley the winds reach speeds of 30 m/s. Thus, from our calculations, it follows that gale-force winds could easily move the stones along the slick clay on the surface of the former lake bed.

### The derivation of formula 5 to the problem "Unusual rocks in the Valley of Death": the force of action of the airflow against an obstacle

We asess the magnitude of the force $F$, exerted by the airflow against an obstacle. For this we use Newton's second law in waveform:

$$F\Delta t = mv, (1)$$

where $v$ is the speed of the airflow; $m$ is the mass of the column of air that impacts the obstacle over time $\Delta t$.

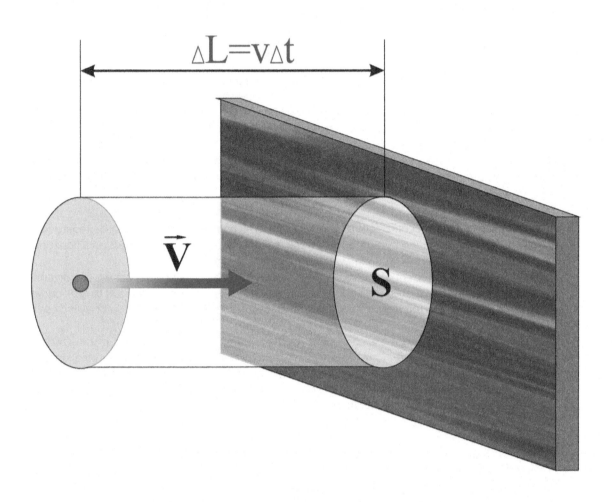

For assessing the impact of the force of the wind

Mass m can be calculated using the formula:

$$m = \rho_{\text{в}} S \Delta L, \quad (2)$$

where $\rho_{\text{в}}$ is air density; $S$ is the cross-sectional area of the air column; $\Delta L$ is the length of the air column that impacts the obstacle over the time $\Delta t$.

The length of the air column $\Delta L$ equals:

$$\Delta L = v \Delta t. \quad (3)$$

And so, the air mass $m$ is equal to:

$$m = \rho_{\text{в}} S v \Delta t. \quad (4)$$

Substituting (4) into (1), we obtain:

$$F = \rho_{\text{в}} S v^2. \quad (5)$$

Please note: We have found that the force of the air flow on the obstacle is proportional to the square   of the flow rate.

## ABOUT THE AUTHORS

**Anatoly Guin** — TRIZ Master, Founder and Head of Research at the International Laboratory Education for a New Era, Vice President of the International Association TRIZ on issues pertaining to primary education, General Director of the autonomous non-profit organization promoting innovation TRIZ-profi, Moscow.

While still a university student, he felt the calling to work in schools. He taught physics to gifted children in an advanced program. Throughout his career he has never ceased working on perfecting teaching methodology. His background also includes work with socially maladapted adolescents. In 1986 he underwent TRIZ training. Since then, began to adapt and apply TRIZ and other methods culled from world practice to find new ideas for the development of creativity of school-aged children.

He has conducted more than 180 workshops for students, teachers, psychologists, university teachers, engineers and entrepreneurs in the CIS countries, Europe and Asia. He has authored more than 10 books which have been published in 12 countries, including the US, France, Japan, China, South Korea.

**Mark Barkan** — Doctor of Technical Sciences and Master of Business Administration, TRIZ Master, Master Black Belt in Lean Six Sigma. In1976, he emigrated to the United States from Kiev, Ukraine. He has served as chief engineer, chief designer and vice president in various companies. In 1991 he became acquainted with TRIZ and joined his future life with this theory.

He has completed about 250 consulting projects applying TRIZ in different industry sectors. In 2005, 2007 and 2009, he was elected President of the International TRIZ Association, MATRIZ. Since 2011 he is serving as Member of the Presidium and the Executive Director of MATRIZ.

In 2007 he began to collaborate closely with Anatoly Guin to promote the practical application of technigues for developing the creative skills of children in the education system. Since 2011, at the request of Anatoly Guin, he became President of the International non-political association Education for a New Era.

# REFERENCES

1. Altshuller, G.S. 2003. Naiti ideyu [Find the idea]. Introduction to the Theory of Inventive Problem Solving – 3rd ed., Supplemented. – Petrozavodsk: Scandinavia.

2. Berezina, V.G. 2001. Vospitanie Chudom – Pedagogika + TRIZ [An Education Marvel – Pedagogy + TRIZ

3. A collection of articles for teachers, educators and education administrators. No. 6 Moscow: VITA-PRESS.

4. Guin, A.A. and A.A. Kartoteka pedagogicheskikh izobretenii b zadach [Files of Pedagogical Inventions and Applications]. – Website for Education for a New Era: http://www.trizway.com/art/cards/33.html.

5. Guin, A.A. 1996. Nas zdut serieznyt izmeneniya v sisteme obucheniya [Major Changes in the Education System Await Us] – Pedagogika + TRIZ: Collection of articles for teachers, educators and education administrators. No. 1 – Gomel: IPP SOZH.

6. Guin, A.A. 2012. Priemy pedagogicheskoi tekhniki: Svobody vybora [Approaches to Educational Technology: Freedom of Choice] Openness. Action. Feedback. Ideanost: Posobie dlya uchitelei [Ideality: Workbook for Teachers.] Moscow: VITA-PRESS.

7. Guin, A.A. 2001. Skola-fabrika umryot. Chto dalshe?: Obrazovanie na smene tsivilizatsii. [The Factory School is Dying. What Next?: Education at the shift in civilizations]. – Pedagogy + TRIZ: Collection of articles for teachers, educators and education administrators. No. 6. Moscow: VITA-PRESS.

8. Ivanov, G.I. 1994. Formuly tvorchestva, ili Kak naucitsya izobretat: Kn. dlya uchaschikhsya st. klassov [Formulas for Creativity, or Teaching How to Invent: Book for High school Students Moscow: Prosveschenie.

9. Merkulov, V.I. 1989. Gidrodinamika znakomaya i nezyakomaya [Known and Unknown Hydrodynamics] Moscow.

10. Mingo, J. 1995. Sekreti uspekha velikikh kompanii (52 istorii iz biznesa i torgovli)[Success Secrets of Great Companies (52 stories from business and trade)]. – SPb.: Piter Press.

11. Murashkovsky, I. and Yu. Murashkovsky "Ya zazheg v svoem serdtse ogon…" ["I lit a fire in my heart"] http://www.trizway.com/art/creative/77.html – Website for Education for a New Era: http://www.trizway.com/art/cards/77.html

12. Ivanov, Dz. 1996. Iskusstvo tvorcheskogo myshleniya [The Art of Creative Thinking]. - Minsk: Potpurri.

FOR CREATIVE IDEAS

FOR CREATIVE IDEAS

CPSIA information can be obtained at www.ICGtesting.com
Printed in the USA
LVOW05s0020240715

447233LV00001B/1/P